Autobiography of Rabindranath Tagore

Parameshwar Hegde
M.Sc., M.A.

Gaurav Book Center
4832/24, Prahlad Lane, S-207 Ansari Raod, Daryaganj, New Delhi-110002

Published by
Gaurav Book Center
4832/24, Prahlad Lane, S-207 Ansari Raod, Daryaganj,
New Delhi-110002
Tel.: 011-43570976, 23278261,
Email-nehapubdistributors@gmail.com

First Edition : 2013

ISBN : 978-93-80317-13-7

Price : 325/-

Laser Typesetting by : Tamalika Computers, Delhi

Printed at: Nagri Printers, Delhi

PRINTED IN INDIA

Published by Gaurav Book Center, New Delhi-110002

Preface

Rabindranath Tagore , sobriquet Gurudev, was an Indian Bengali polymath. He was a popular poet, novelist, musician, and playwright who reshaped Bengali literature and music in the late 19th and early 20th centuries. As author of *Gitanjali* and its "profoundly sensitive, fresh and beautiful verse", and as the first Asian to win the Nobel Prize in Literature, Tagore was perhaps the most widely regarded Indian literary figure of all time. He was a mesmerizing representative of the Indian culture whose influence and popularity internationally perhaps could only be compared to that of Gandhi, whom Tagore named 'Mahatma' out of his deep admiration for him.

A Pirali Brahmin from Kolkata, Tagore was already writing poems at age eight. At age sixteen, he published his first substantial poetry under the pseudonym *Bhanushingho* ("Sun Lion") and wrote his first short stories and dramas in 1877. Tagore denounced the British Raj and supported independence. His efforts endure in his vast canon and in the institution he founded, Visva-Bharati University.

Tagore modernised Bengali art by spurning rigid classical forms. His novels, stories, songs, dance-dramas, and essays spoke to political and personal topics. *Gitanjali* (*Song Offerings*), *Gora* (*Fair-Faced*), and *Ghare-Baire* (*The Home and the World*) are his best-known works, and his verse, short stories, and novels were acclaimed for their lyricism, colloquialism, naturalism, and contemplation. Tagore was perhaps the only litterateur who penned anthems of two countries: India and Bangladesh: *Jana Gana Mana* and *Amar Shonar Bangla*.

Tagore's last four years were marked by chronic pain and two long periods of illness. These began when Tagore lost consciousness in late 1937; he remained comatose and near death for an extended period. This was followed three years later, in late 1940, by a similar spell, from which he never recovered. The poetry Tagore wrote in these years is among his finest, and is distinctive for its preoccupation with death. After extended suffering, Tagore died on 7 August 1941 (22 Shravan 1348) in an upstairs room of the Jorasanko mansion in which he was raised; his death anniversary is mourned across the Bengali-speaking world.

Via translations, Tagore influenced Hispanic literature: Chileans Pablo Neruda and Gabriela Mistral, Mexican writer Octavio Paz, and Spaniards José Ortega y Gasset, Zenobia Camprubí, and Juan Ramón Jiménez. Between 1914 and 1922, the Jiménez-Camprubí spouses translated twenty-two of Tagore's books from English into Spanish and extensively revised and adapted such works as Tagore's *The Crescent Moon*. In this time, Jiménez developed "naked poetry" (Spanish: «poesia desnuda»), a landmark innovation. Ortega y Gasset wrote that "Tagore's wide appeal [may stem from the fact that] he speaks of longings for perfection that we all have ... Tagore awakens a dormant sense of childish wonder, and he saturates the air with all kinds of enchanting promises for the reader, who ... pays little attention to the deeper import of Oriental mysticism". Tagore's works circulated in free editions around 1920 alongside those of Dante Alighieri, Miguel de Cervantes, Johann Wolfgang von Goethe, Plato, and Leo Tolstoy.

Tagore was deemed overrated by some Westerners. Graham Greene doubted that "anyone but Mr. Yeats can still take his poems very seriously." Modern remnants of a past Latin American reverence of Tagore were discovered, for example, by an astonished Salman Rushdie during a trip to Nicaragua.

Parameshwar Hegde
M.Sc.,M.A.

Contents

1

RABINDRANATH TAGORE AS A PAINTER

Over one thousand poems; nearly two dozen plays and playlets; eight novels; eight or more volumes of short stories; more than two thousands songs, of which he wrote both the words and the music; and a mass of prose on literary, social, religious, political, and other topics. On top of these, his English translations; his paintings; his travels and lecture-tours in Asia, America, and Europe; and his activities as educationist, as social and religious reformer, and politician. The life's work of Ravindranath Tagore is the accomplishment of a titan.

Gurudev Rabindranath Tagore - mystic, visionary, painter and Nobel laureate for literature- was India's grand old man of letters. But Tagore has been immortalised not only by his poetry but also by his paintings and his important contribution to Indian Art through Viswa-Bharati.

Born in Jorasanko on 7th May 1861, seventh in a family of fourteen. The Tagores were a cultured and wealthy family, and Rabindranath's father, Devendranath, was one of the leaders of the Brahma Samaj. The poet's early life was spent in an atmosphere of religion and arts, principally literature, music and painting. In religion his inspiration was derived from the Vedas and the Upanishads, but with him as with many Hindus the Upanisadic monoism was diversified by the Vaisnava dualism.

Rabindranath learnt drawing in his childhood and was attracted to the sketches drawn by his elder brother Jyotirindranath. At the age of seventeen, his first book of poems was published. In 1878, he went to England for further studies but returned back in just seventeen months as he was disappointed with the studies. In music Tagore's training was classical Indian, though as a composer he rebelled against the tyranny of classical orthodoxy, and introduced many variations of form and phrase, notably from Bengali folk-music.

In 1911, on revisiting England, Tagore brought the English Gitanjali, which was published in 1912. Gitanjali saw him winning, in 1913, at the age of 52, the Nobel Prize for literature. The first Nobel prize ever awarded to an Asiatic, made him world-famous. Following this, he was knighted by the British in 1915.

In 1917, Tagore founded the innovative 'Viswa-Bharati' university in the rural settings of Shantiniketan, thus realizing a life-long dream- to create a context for a genuine all-round development of human faculties. Far from the neurosis of the city life, this was not to be a degree-oriented establishment, but an attempt, in his own words "to study the mind of Man in it's realization of different aspects of truth from diverse points of view."

Two years later, in protest against the ghastly massacre of hundreds of innocent Indians at the 'Jallianwallah Bagh' by Genral Dyer, Sir Ravindranath returned his title to the British and quietly opened the art wing of his university called 'Kala Bhavan'. He invited the like-minded painter Nandlal Bose to run the wing with a free hand, thus encouraging the evolution of an original vision, reflecting the intuition and expression of the students, unleashed from the bounds of tradition and the stifling rigours of conventional training. The opening of the 'Kala Bhavan' proved to be a decisive landmark in the history of evolution of Indian Art.

Tagore spent the rest of his life at Santiniketan, except for several travels and lecture-tours in which he carried his message of human integrity to many countries in Asia, America and Europe.

In 1924, while writing "Purabi" he started doodling on the pages of his manuscript. However, Rabindra Nath Tagore's famous world appearance as painter in France in 1930 was not sudden. Long before the Paris exhibition which vaulted him to worldwide painterly fame, in 1926, Tagore had long discussions on his art with Romain Rolland. Himself a Nobel laureate Romain Rolland wrote in his book 'Inde-journal', on 3rd July, 1926 "......other day Tagore was discussing on his application of colour in paintings. He likes very little red colour, the dominance of red colour in Italian village did not attract him. His love goes violet and blue. and he has more liking for green." Tagore had discussions about art with another Nobel Laureate, French poet Saint John Perse over their several meetings in 1920's.

Rabindranath transformed his lack of formal training of art into an advantage and opened new horizons in the use of line and colour. He was prolific in his paintings and sketches as he was in his writing, producing over 2500 of these within a decade. Over 1500 of them are preserved in Viswa-Bharati, Santiniketan.

It is evident that in his search of newer form of expression in line and colour Rabindranath was trying to express something different from what he did in his poetry and songs. If he sought peace and enlightenment in his songs, he seems to explore darkness and mystery in his drawings. Dark creatures and haunting landscapes of another, primordial and marvelous world, which constituted Tagore's works puzzle and delight the world. With the passage of time, critics and art lovers have been discovering in these outpourings from the depths of his fanciful mind a more modern and disquieting Tagore than they see elsewhere.

Tagore himself, in his article 'My Pictures', explains his paintings as follows "The world of sound is a tiny bubble in the silence of the infinite. The Universe has its only language of gesture, it talks in the voice of pictures and dance. Every object in this world proclaims in the dumb signal of lines and colours, the fact that it is not a mere logical abstraction or a mere thing of use, but it is unique in itself, it carries the miracle of its existence. In a picture the artist creates the language of undoubted reality, and we are satisfied that we see. It may not be the representation of a beautiful woman but that of a common place donkey or of something that has no external credential of truth in nature but only in its own inner artistic significance.

"People often ask me about the meaning of my pictures. I remain silent even as my pictures are. It is for them to express and not to explain. They have nothing ulterior behind their own appearance for the thoughts to explore and words to describe, and that appearance carries its ultimate worth. Then they remain, otherwise they are rejected and forgotten even though they may have some scientific truth or ethical justification. Love is kindred to art, it is inexplicable. Duty can be measured by the degree of its benefit, utility by the profit and power it may bring, but art by nothing but itself. There are other factors of life which are visitors that come and go. Art is the guest that comes and remains. The dithers may be important, but Art is inevitable."

In spring 1930, when on a tour to France, Tagore was advised, by some art critics of local newspapers who saw his paintings, to hold an exhibition in Paris. He held the first public and international exhibition of his paintings in Paris in May 1930, at the Gallerie Pigalle. The exhibition was later held in different countries in Europe in the same year. But India and his home town Calcutta had the honour of hosting it only in 1931, a year later of Paris exhibition.

The exhibition remained open to public from the 5th to the 19th May, 1930. Duchess Anna de Noailles, in her introductory remarks in the catalogue of the exhibition of Tagore's paintings "To me it is like climbing a staircase of dreamland"

After the conclusion of Paris exhibition, exhibitions were held in England, Denmark, Sweden, Rome, Germany and Russia in Europe. Later exhibitions were also held in USA and Canada. The exhibition of paintings drew an unprecedented overwhelming admiration in Germany. It was shown in Berlin, Munich, Hamburg, Dusseldorf, Stuttgart and other places in Germany. The then German President and ministers and also Albert Einstein, the great scientist, attended Tagore's exhibition.

Tagore's paintings and sketches fascinated young German students to mass hysteria. Among them a student of the Art Academy of Munich Oswald Malura, at the age of 20, received a Mond travel scholarship of the academy to study Indian art and philosophy. Malura stayed in India for three years (1929-1932) and visited Bombay, Agra, Delhi, Kashmir, Benaras, Himalayas, Santiniketan and Calcutta and he met Annie Besant, Mahatma Gandhi and poet Tagore.

At Santiniketan, this amateur cinematogarpher recorded a 12 minute-film on Tagore as a painter and teacher in the open-air classes. There are some still photographs that showed how Tagore drew and painted but this movie film or cinema on Tagore as an artist is indeed rare.

Malura revisited Calcutta in 1986 and presented this short silent film on Tagore as painter to the Visva Bharati University in December 1986. Mr. Malura said, "my impression was that Tagore was to me like a Godsent man. I liked so much his sketches and colouring that I could not resist myself to photograph it. But alas! it was in black and white."

In Tagore's own words, "The world speaks to me in colours, my soul answers in music". Obviously, the soul was very articulate with colours too.

In later years, as Tagore reached his sixties, he tried to finance his Vishwa-Bharati University personally, relying on royalties and proceeds from his lecture tours. By 1941, Tagore's health had seriously deteriorated. Tagore died peacefully, after an operation in Calcutta on August 7, 1941.

In his life, he embodied the quintessence of Indian culture, combining an abundant intellect with a devout passion to his cause, and his inspirational compositions have stood the passage of time. Tagore's contribution to the art of India remains one of the most important till date.

Tagore is well known for his poetry works, but very few know that he was also a man of actions. His works focused on certain issues such as racial humiliation, search for self-esteem, education, and religion that was concerned with India. Two songs from his rabindrasangeet canon are now the national anthems of Bangladesh and India: the Amar Shonar Bangla and the Jana Gana Mana. Tagore was also a cultural reformer and polymath who modernised Bengali art by rejecting strictures binding it to classical Indian forms. Literary works, nationalism and Santiniketan remianed the passions of Tagore for more than six decades of his life.Tagore breathed his last in the year 1941.

His early days: Tagore was born the youngest of fourteen children in the Jorasanko

mansion of parents Debendranath Tagore and Sarada Devi.Rabindranath Tagore was born in a family that could easily be passed off as one of the leading Indian merchants. The Tagores were a cultured and wealthy family, and Rabindranath's father, Debendranath, was one of the leaders of the Brahma Samaj. Rabindranath's family was a blend of the Hindu and British culture. Rabindranath Tagore was born at a time that he described as: "the modern city-bred spirit of progress that had just begin to drive its triumphal car over the luscious green life of our ancient village community". In other words, Rabindranath was born in an atmosphere of the advent of new Bengali ideals. Rabindranath's progressive views and ideals can be attributed to his family's belief in synthesis of old and new influences. The poet's early life was spent in an atmosphere of religion and arts, principally literature, music and painting. Tagore's philosophies and way of living was heavily influenced by the Vedic and Upanishadic concepts. In music Tagore's training was classical Indian, though as a composer he rebelled against the tyranny of classical orthodoxy, and introduced many variations of form and phrase, notably from Bengali folk music of the Baul and Bhatiyali type. Rabindranath wrote his first poem at the age of six and as a young boy studied the classical poetry of Kalidasa. He also studied the Upanishads, languages and modern sciences. He did his basic education at home. His home schooling, life in Shilaidaha, and travels made Tagore a nonconformist and pragmatist. However seeking to become a barrister, Tagore enrolled at a public school in Brighton, England in 1878; later, he studied at University College London, but returned to Bengal in 1880 without a degree.

His foray into literature: Rabindranath's earlier works reflected his belief in his own country and in a culture of universal humanity transcending all barriers of time and place. He published his first substantial poetry-under the pseudonym Bhanushingho ("Sun Lion") -in 1877 and wrote his first short stories and dramas at age sixteen.This self-expression of Rabindranath Tagore became apparent especially between 1878-80. This was the period when the national movement coincided with the neo-Hindu revival in Bengal. If on one level he criticized the caste system and rituals through his poems and writings, then on the other level he tried to justify its existence. During the Swadeshi movement, Rabindranath wrote several books, articles, poems and songs about Bengal that then created a patriotic fervor. Some of his famous works at that time included an essay called 'Swadeshi Samaj' and a famous novel called 'Gora' and short stories like 'Kabuli Walla'. Rabindranath pointed out that his brothers set a bold example by strongly advocating Bengali literature at a time when the educated men began to keep at arms length both the language and the thought of their native land. It can hence be noted that his brothers were the inspiration for Rabindranath at the onset of his literary career.

Rabindranath as a Poet: Rabindranath Tagore was known for his different forms of creative writing such as essays, letters, short stories, novels and dramas and is best known for his poems. Among his fifty and odd volumes of poetry are Manasi (1890) [The Ideal One], Sonar Tari (1894) [The Golden Boat], Gitanjali (1910) [Song Offerings], Gitimalya (1914) [Wreath of Songs], and Balaka (1916) [The Flight of Cranes]. The English renderings of his poetry, which include The Gardener (1913), Fruit-Gathering (1916), and The Fugitive (1921), do not generally correspond to particular volumes in the original Bengali; and in spite of its title, Gitanjali: Song Offerings (1912), the most acclaimed of them, contains poems from other works besides its namesake. Tagore's major plays are Raja (1910) [The King of the Dark Chamber], Dakghar (1912) [The Post Office], Achalayatan (1912) [The Immovable], Muktadhara (1922) [The Waterfall], and Raktakaravi (1926) [Red Oleanders]. His poems reflected his beliefs and his feelings, be it of protest against wrong done or of support for a humanitarian cause. Tagore's poetry was influenced by traditional Indian poetry. For example, the devotional Indian poets of Ramprasad and Kabir especially influenced his early poetry works. Later he was influenced by the Baoul tradition, which is a tradition of traditional Bengali folk music, known for its simple ballads and invocation to union with the beloved. He won a Nobel Prize too for his poetic work- Gitanjali (song offering). So much was Rabindranath's dedication towards his work that it is believed that only hours before he died on August 7, in 1941, Tagore dictated his last poem. Infact his critics say that he wrote some of his finest poetry and drama in the final decade of his life from 1930 to 1940. They term this period as the 'Last Harvest'.

Life at Santiniketan: By 1863 Rabindranath turned his attention to the Santiniketan School after withdrawing from the Swadeshi movement. Later on, Rabindranath founded the Santiniketan School in his father's ashram in 1901. Santiniketan was located within two miles of the Bolpur railway station on the East Indian Railway line. The school had the advantage of being situated in the heart of nature but not too far from the city. In his school, he set out to resurrect the best things in the Indian inheritance, but gave it a universal humanist outlook. He hoped to give life to the Upanishadic concept in his Santiniketan institution. Rabindranath was convinced that all human problems such as poverty, religious discord, and disunity would find their resolution in education. Happiness and freedom were the two fundamental principles of Santiniketan. The arrangements at Santiniketan were extremely primitive. However, soon Rabindranath realized that a Brahmacharya Ashram was not his idea of a new and modern education. Though he valued the primitive nature of Santiniketan, his ideal school had to do much more than that, especially with regard to opening up the student's minds to a relationship with the world. In the year 1918, Rabindranath Tagore established Santiniketan College, which later on in 1926 had to be affiliated to University of Calcutta. Step by step Santiniketan moved from being a collection of separate educational experiments into a well-knit whole- a school, a college, a department of higher studies and research, a center of art and music.

Nobel Prize and life beyond: "Gitanjali (Song Offered) was not simply an Indian voice, strange and far, but it was also our voice". -W.B Yeats.

This was the remark made by poet W.B Yeats after reading Tagore's award winning poem Gitanjali. It all began with Rothenstein who found the poems of Rabindranath Tagore interesting and sent them to renowned poet W.B. Yeats. He invited a group of culturally influential friends to dinner at a restaurant in London on 10th July 1912 where Yeats presided. The dinner was followed by an evening in Rothenstein's house where Yeats recited Rabindranath's poems. Those present were charmed and unanimously appreciated the work. Soon afterwards Yeats and Rothenstein worked together to publish a private edition of the English Gitanjali through the India Society of London. Even before the Nobel Prize was announced, Gitanjali became widely accepted all over. The poem was read at several literary felicitations. Finally the news of the Nobel Prize reached him on 13th November 1913. After this episode Rabindranath came to be known as bilingual author. He won the award for the English translation of the poem. In the summer of 1912, Rabindranath took to England some translations of his favourite poems. He did the translations when recuperating from a bout of ill health. The Nobel Committee gave Tagore the prize:

> "Because of his profoundly sensitive, fresh and beautiful verse, by which, with consummate skill, he has made his poetic thought, expressed in his own English words, a part of the literature of the West".

This prestigious award brought Tagore into the public eye in both the East and West. He later on often traveled to the U.S and Europe to share his poetry and raise funds for his own ashram.

After winning the award, there was a great demand for his work in English. In response to that demand he put together more and more translations of his writings. Rabindranath's poetry became a part of England's literary canon, but predictably, and as anticipated by the poet himself, his post-Gitanjali work did not attract the same interest. Tagore was also awarded the knighthood in 1915, but he surrendered it in 1919 as a protest against the Massacre of Amritsar, where British troops killed some 400 Indian demonstrators protesting colonial laws.

His last years: Rabindranath Tagore, who died in 1941 at the age of eighty, is a towering figure in the millennium-old literature of Bengal. Anyone who becomes familiar with this large and flourishing tradition will be impressed by the power of Tagore's presence in Bangladesh and in India. His poetry as well as his novels, short stories, and essays are very widely read, and the songs he composed reverberate around the eastern part of India and throughout Bangladesh.In contrast, in the rest of the world, especially in Europe and America, the excitement that Tagore's writings created in the early years of the twentieth century has largely vanished.Tagore's last four years

(1937-1941) were marked by chronic pain and two long periods of illness. The poetry Tagore wrote in these twilight years are distinctive for their preoccupation with death; these more profound and mystical experimentations allowed Tagore to be branded a "modern poet". There never was a poet more of the earth, earthier, than Tagore. The beauty and splendor of the earth he has proudly and lovingly sung in many a poem. His final lecture, Crisis in Civilization was read on his eightieth birthday. Rabindranath passed away in the same house in which he was born.

2

BENGALI POETRY

Like the Bengali language, Bengali poetry traces its lineage to Pali and other Prakrit socio-cultural traditions. An antagonism to Vedic rituals and laws heightened to a culmination in the Buddhist and Jainist movements. However, modern Bengali owes as much to Sanskrit. Like the society that thrived to populate the modern Bengal, Bengali language and culture appears to be a perfect amalgam of almost unanalysable elements.

The period between 1350 and 1800 was the Medieval period of Bengali poetry. It was known as the period of Jayadeva (12th century), the renowned poet from neighboring Orissa, famous for his magnum opus Gitagovinda. Vidyapati (13th century) with his love lyrics, and Badu Chandidas, the author of Sri Krishna Kirtan, the most important philosophical ang most erotic work of the period. The period from 1500 A.D. to 1800 A.D. was known as the Late Middle Bengali period. During this period, there was a marked influence of Chaitanya, which led to the development of Vaishnava literature. Chandidas (13th century) is one of the greatest poets of this time. Other Vaishnava poets include Govinddas and Gyandas.

Bharat Chandra probably marks the transition period of precolonial theocentric poetry and modern poetry. After Bharat Chandra there is a long list of poets notable Iswar Gupta before Michael Madhusudan Dutta (1834–1873) who is the founder of modern age of Bengali literature. Another great poet of this period is Biharilal Chakravarti's (1834–94). Then Rabindranath

Tagore(1861–1941), Kazi Nazrul Islam (1899–1976), Jatindramohan Bagchi (1878–1948) and many others begin the age of modern bengali poetry.

With Rabindranath founding a firm basis for Bengali poetry, the new poets of the early 1920s started a conscious movement for transcending the frontiers of traditional verses and establishing a realm of truly 'modern' poetry in Bengali. It was a successful movement that brought permanent change about the concept of structure of poetry, in addition to theme. One notable sect of modernists included pro-socialism poets like Sukanta Bhattacharya and Samar Sen.

The modern age begins with a group of writers who wrote for Kallol, a modernist movement magazine (Little magazine movement), founded in 1923. The most popular among the group were Kazi Nazrul Islam (1899–1976) and Mohitlal Majumder (1888–1952), Achintyakumar Sengupta (1903–1976), Satyendranath Dutta (1882–1922), Premendra Mitra (1904–1988) and others . Then Bengali poetry got into the brightest light of modernism in 1930s, through the movement of few other little magazines, such as Buddhadeb Bosu's *Kabita* and Sudhindranath Datta's *Parichay* .

The great poets of those movements— Jibanananda Das (1899–1954), Buddhadev Bose (1908–1974), Sudhindranath Dutta (1901–1960), Bishnu Dey (1909–1982), Amiya Chakravarty (1901–1986) and Samar Sen (1916–1987) were the main characters who made a significant effort to reshape Bengali Poetry.

The Hungryalist movement, also known as Hungry generation was launched from the Patna residence of Malay Roy Choudhury by Shakti Chattopadhyay, Samir Roychoudhury and Haradhon Dhara alias Debi Ray in November 1961 with the publication of a manifesto on poetry. Subsequently more than 30 poets, writers and painters joined the movement. The movement was disbanded in 1965 when some of the Hungryalists were arrested for their anti-establishment writings. Malay Roy Choudhury was jailed by the lower court, though Kolkata High Court exonerated him. The movement had a lasting impact inasmuch as it changed the literary trend and caused a little magazine explosion in Bengali literature.

Bengali poetry since early seventies got a new impetus in the hands of a group of poets who contributed a lot in terms of ideas and poetic diction of their own. The poets are Ananya Roy, Tushar Chowdhury,Ranajit Das, Kamal Chakraborty, Mridul Dasgupta,Syed Kawsar Jamal,Ujjal Singha, Jamil Syed,Joy Goswami and others.

Later since the mid 80's Bengali Literature experienced a new genre of Bengali poetry called New Poetry. From the early 90's with impetus from a Kolkata based poetry journal Kabita Campus, New Poetry has began to gain immense acclamation from young contemporary poets of Bengal. In 2003 some poets of this genre have started a journal named Natun Kabita containing their ideas and poems, through, both, online and print media. Another new age poetry magazine in the same sphere is Boikhoribhashya. Poets associated with this literary movement are:

Barin Ghosal, Ranjan Maitra, Swapan Roy, Dhiman Chakraborty, Alok Biswas, Pronob Pal, Saumitra Sengupta, Arupratan Ghosh, Indranil Ghosh, Amitava Praharaj and Debanjan Das. Rajarshi Chattopadhyay, Atanu Bandopadhyay, Pradip Chakraborty are poets who joined this movement in the mid 90's.

The first decade of this century (2000–09) is considered to be the period of a New Age Little Magazine Movement . The magazines prominent in this period are:

Sanjbati, Lalon, Bodhshabda, Pratishedhak, Dolchhut, Abosardanga, Ashtray, Ahir, Byas etc. Gouri Sankar Bandyopadhyay ('Madhya Chaitre Mailbox', Prativash, June 2009)

Major poets rising from the period are:

Sankha Subhra Devbarman, Aritra Sanyal, Atanu Singha, Animikh Patra, Souptik Chakraborty, Somtirtha Nandi, Susnata Jana, Tanmay Mandal, Souva Chattopadhyay, Arindam Ray,

Deb Maity, Sayantan Mukhopadhyay, Saibal Sarkar, Arup Ghosh, Himalay Jana, Kaushik Bhowmik, Anamitra Roy, Rohon Kuddus, Sanghamitra Haldar, Himadri Mukhopadhyay, Somnath Ghosal, Swadesh Misra, Swagata Dasgupta, Nabendu Bikash Ray, Paramita Das

Gitanjali

Gitanjali is a collection of 103 English poems, largely translations, by the Bengali poet Rabindranath Tagore. This volume became very famous in the West, and was widely translated.

Gitanjali is also the title of an earlier Bengali volume (1910) of 157 mostly devotional songs. The word *gitanjoli* is composed from "git", song, and "anjoli", offering, and thus means - "An offering of songs"; but the word for offering, *anjoli,* has a strong devotional connotation, so the title may also be interpreted as "prayer offering of song".

The English collection is not a translation of poems from the Bengali volume of the same name. While half the poems (52 out of 103) in the English text were selected from the Bengali volume, others were taken from these works (given with year and number of songs selected for the English text): *Gitimallo* (1914,17), *Noibeddo* (1901,15), *Khea* (1906,11) and a handful from other works. The translations were often radical, leaving out or altering large chunks of the poem and in one instance even fusing two separate poems (song 95, which unifies songs 89,90 of naivedya).

The translations were undertaken prior to a visit to England in 1912, where the poems were extremely well received. A slender volume was published in 1913, with an exhilarating preface by W. B. Yeats. In the same year, based on a corpus of three thin translations, Rabindranath became the first non-European to win the Nobel prize.

The poems of Gitanjali express a largely metaphysical outlook, talking about a union with the "supreme"; but like much western poetry that explores similar themes, the language suggests the union of two earthly lovers. This type of anthropomorphic depiction of celestial love is quite common in the Vaishnava literature of India since the 12th c. (see Vidyapati or Jayadeva). Rabindranath Tagore encountered it also in his interactions with the Baul community in rural Bengal. For example, poem 7 in the English volume renders poem 125 from the Bengali gItanjali, *Amar e gan chherechhe tar shôkol ôlongkar* and talks of heavenly love in terms of the lover taking off her jewelry, which is getting in the way of the union. See also the poem 18, at the bottom of this page.

Some poems involve themes related to nature, but here, too, the spiritual is subtly present, as in this poem (no. 57), given here along with the Bangla text in Roman script:

Light, my light, the world-filling light, the eye-kissing light, heart-sweetening light!

Ah, the light dances, my darling, at the centre of my life; the light strikes, my darling, the chords of my love; the sky opens, the wind runs wild, laughter passes over the earth.

The butterflies spread their sails on the sea of light. Lilies and jasmines surge up on the crest of the waves of light.

The light is shattered into gold on every cloud, my darling, and it scatters gems in profusion.

Mirth spreads from leaf to leaf, my darling, and gladness without measure. The heaven's river has drowned its banks and the flood of joy is abroad.

Alo amar, alo ogo, alo bhubon bhora
alo noyon dhoa amar, alo hridoe hara.
Nache alo nache, o bhai, amar praner kachhe —
baje alo baje, o bhai, hridoe binar majhe —
jage akash, chhote batash, hashe shokol dhora.
Alor srote pal tulechhe hajar projapoti.
Alor dheue uthlo mete mollika maloti.
Meghe meghe shona, o bhai, jae na manik gona —
patae patae hashi, o bhai, pulok rashi rashi.
Shuronodir kul ?ubechhe shudha-nijhor-jhora.

-Ocholaeoton

In the English-speaking world, the writings of Tagore are no longer widely read. Nonetheless, for millions of Bangla speakers, the Bengali originals continue to resonate, as in this verse:

I stand mesmerized,
wondering how you sing
your notes hold the world spellbound -
the light of your music
lights up my universe.

(song 22 of Bengali Gitanjali, song 3 in the English.)

3

VISVA BHARATI UNIVERSITY

Visva Bharati University, Santiniketan is a Central University for research and teaching in India, located in the twin town of Santiniketan and Sriniketan Indian state of West Bengal. It was founded by Rabindranath Tagore who called it *Visva Bharati,* which means the communion of the world with India. In its initial years Tagore expressed his dissatisfaction with the word 'university', since university translates to *Vishva-Vidyalaya,* which is smaller in scope than *Visva Bharati.* Until independence it was a college. Soon after independence, in 1951 the institution was given the status of a university, and was renamed *Visva Bharati University.*

The origins of the university date back to 1863 when Maharshi Debendranath Tagore, himself the *zamindar* of Silaidaha in East Bengal, bought a tract of land from the *zamindar* of Raipur, which was a neighbouring village not too far from present day Santiniketan and set up an *ashram* at the spot that has now come to be called *chatim tala* at the heart of the town. The *ashram* was initially called *Brahmacharya Ashram,* which was later renamed *Brahmacharya Vidyalaya.* It was established with a view to encourage people from all walks of life to come to the spot and meditate. In 1901 his youngest son Rabindranath Tagore established a co-educational school inside the premises of the *ashram.*

From 1901 onwards, Tagore used the *ashram* to organise the *Hindu Mela*, which soon became a centre of nationalist activity. Through the early twentieth century the former *zamindars* of Surul, another neighbouring village, a few minutes by cycle from the Uttarayan Complex, continued to accede their lands and other properties to the *ashram* and the college that was being built on this spot. On 23 December 1921 Tagore formally started the college with proceeds from the prize money of the Nobel Prize he received in 1913 for the publication of his book of poems entitled *Gitanjali*. The college also became a centre of Brahmo learning in this period. It was granted full university status in May 1951 by the Government of independent India. The poet's eldest son, Rathindranath Tagore, became the first *upacharya* of the newly founded university. Another member of the Tagore family who performed the role of *upacharya* of the university was Indira Devi Chaudhurani, a niece of the poet.

The high officials of the university include the *Paridarshaka* (Visitor), *Acharya* (Chancellor), and the *Upacharya* (Vice Chancellor). The *Paridarshaka* of this university is the President of India, while the *Acharya* is the Prime Minister of India. The university is run by its *Karma Samity* (Executive Council) which is chaired by the *Acharya*. The institutes and departments are located in both Santiniketan and Sriniketan.

The university is divided in to institutes, centres, departments and schools. The respective departments are included in the institutes. The university's various programmes dealing with its rich cultural heritage as well as art and dance education are funded by the Department of Science and Technology (DST), Government of India.

Institutes and Museums

Cheena Bhavana (Institute of Chinese Language and Culture): It was founded in April 1937 with the great vision of Tagore. Tagore invited Prof. Tan Yunshan to serve as the first chairperson of *Cheena Bhavana*. International scholars such as Jan Yun-hua worked at the Cheena-Bhavana on topics ranging from

Sino-Indian studies, Buddhism and Chinese philosophy. Chiang Kai-shek and Zhou Enlai donated a large number of Chinese books to *Cheena Bhavan*, making it one of the most important libraries for classical Chinese studies in India.

***Darshan Bhavana* (Institute of Philosophy)**: This department is also well-known for its research and teaching. Professor Jiten Mohanty has been associated with the work of this department.

***Kala Bhavana* (Institute of Fine Arts)**: Arguably one of the most well known of all the departments of the university, it boasts of an extremely well known faculty and students' body. It is most well known for the spread of Bengal School of Art. Abanindranath Tagore, one of India's most eminent artists was one of its founders and chief patrons. Luminaries such as Abanindranath Tagore, Gaganendranath Tagore, Nandalal Bose, Binode Bihari Mukherjee, Ramkinkar Baij, Dinkar Kaushik, K.G. Subramanyan and Ghulam Mohammed Sheikh have either taught or been students here.

Silpa-Sadana has a long tradition in the production of artistic and innovative products. It carries tremendous potentialities in Socio-economical values in today's context. The vision is also to bring rural people into the economic mainstream without uprooting them from their roots the focus is on 'product diversification' and the products developed in classrooms would go to the craftsmen trained in the Certificate course for production. The products made are available for sale at Silpa Sadana Emporium. Design intervention is integral part of the learning process this is done through classroom projects, workshops, exhibitions and interaction between artisans of different community & states etc. Presently Silpa Sadana offers various training programs including:

Bachelor of Design (B. Des) of 4 years duration after 12th in any stream with in 25 years in: Textiles & Accessories Pottery/ Ceramics & Accessories Furniture & life style products (12 seats each)

Certificate courses of 2 years duration after 10th without any age bar in: Hand-made paper, Batik work, Leather crafts, Handloom weaving, wood work, Pottery.

Short term Courses of 8- 20 weeks without age bar admission open through out the year in: Traditional Batik & Bandhni, Clay Jewelry, Ceramics Table ware, Ceramics Tiles, Creative Weaving (Tapestry & Hobby Loom), Dyeing & Printing, Glazing and Firing, Paper Pulp & Hand- Made Paper craft, Leather crafts, Natural Dyes, Raku Craft, Terracotta Craft, Wooden Toy, Wooden Jewelry, Wood Carving, Wood Turning. (4 seats each)

Girls and Boys Hostel accommodation is available close to the Institute.

Bengal Institute of technology and Management (BITM, Santiniketan) IIIT, Kolkata

Both these institutes are now affiliated with the WBUT (West Bengal University of Technology), which was formed to bring all engineering education under different universities in West Bengal under a single umbrella. IIIT Kolkata (International Institute of Information Technology) was renamed to IERCEM Institute of Information Technology after its affiliation with the WBUT.

Schools

Patha Bhavana: It is not only the oldest school of the university, but also the oldest institution on which the university was subsequently built. It is the university school of Santiniketan. Initially called *Ashram Vidyalaya* it was also later called *Santiniketan Vidyalaya*. It was started by Tagore in 1901. The distinctive features of this co-educational school include its open air classrooms and emphasis upon oriental learning. The school, being the nucleus of the university and the town is within the *Santiniketan Ashram*. The first four students of the school included Tagore's son Rathindranath Tagore, the first *Upacharya* of the university and Sudhi Ranjan Das, a Chief Justice of India. The future Nobel Laureate in economics, Amartya

Sen completed his school education from this school. So did one of the first Indian Rhodes Scholars, Asim Datta. Supriyo Tagore, a great grandson of Satyendranath Tagore, the eldest brother of the poet, was one of its longest serving and most well known Principals. The eminent historians, Tapan Raychaudhuri and Ashin Dasgupta have periodically taken classes here.

Mrinalini Ananda Pathsala: Founded in 1954 it was named after Rabindranath Tagore's wife Mrinalini Devi. It is a preparatory school for *Patha Bhavana*. It is housed in the *Notun Bari* and *Dehali*.

Santosh Pathsala: Founded in 1988 it is kindergarten school named after Santosh Chandra Majumdar. It is a preparatory school for *Shiksha Shastra*.

Shiksha Shatra: It was founded in 1924. It was later shifted to Sriniketan in 1927. The students of this school are from the neighbouring villages.

Uttar Shiksha Sadana: This school was started in 1976.

The twin towns of Santiniketan and Sriniketan are surrounded by Bolpur to the north, Kheya to the south, Surul to the east and Prantik to the west. The towns and the university are situated not too far away from the river *Kopai* which flows to the south. This university is especially famous for its cultural festivals. These festivals are as follows:

(1) ***Basanta Utsab*** (**Spring Festival**): This festival is identified with *doljatra* or *holi*, which is held on the grounds in front of *Patha Bhavana*.

(2) ***Poush Mela*** (**Winter Fair**): It is the annual winter fair which is held every *Poush* which coincides with December on *Purono Melar Maath* opposite the *ashram* and next to the *Uttarayan* complex, as well as on *Melar Maath* (*Bhubandangar Maath*), which is next to the administrative block. The fair is meant to encourage the local people of Birbhum and outlying other districts of Bengal to come and exhibit and sell their wares. *Jatras,* such as Alkap, are staged and Bouls perform at the fair.

On the first day of the fair, i.e. 23 December, the university organises a *Upasana Sabha* at *Chatimtala* (under a Chatim tree), the spot where Maharshi Debendranath Tagore came and established his *ashram* for the first time in 1863. On 24 December the university organises a display of lights and fireworks on *Melar Maath,* a custom started by the poet, Rabindranath Tagore himself. On Christmas Day, the university organises the *Christo Utsab,* which is meant as a mark of respect for all religions.

4

DEBENDRANATH TAGORE

Debendranath Tagore 15 May 1817 – 19 January 1905) was the founder in 1848 of the Brahmo Religion which today is synonymous with Brahmoism the youngest religion of India and Bangladesh.

A Bengali, he was born in Calcutta, India. His father, was the fabulous "Prince" Dwarkanath Tagore.

Debendranath was a deeply religious man. His movement the Brahmo Samaj was formed in 1843 by merging his Tattwabodhini Sabha with the Brahmo Sabha, ten years after the death of the latter's founder, Raja Ram Mohan Roy. The Brahmo Sabha had fallen away from its original practices put forth in its Trust deed of Brahmo Sabha, however, Tagore revived the importance of this deed.

Debendranath's spiritual prowess was of the highest order, even while he maintained his worldly affairs – not renouncing his material possessions as some Hindu traditions prescribed but rather continuing to enjoy them in a spirit of detachment. His considerable material property included several estates spread over the districts of Bengal; most famously, the later acquisition Santiniketan estate near Bolpur in the Birbhum district where his eldest son Dwijendranath Tagore set up his school.

Debendranath was a master of the Upanishads and played no small role in the education and cultivation of faculties of his sons.

Dwijendranath (1840–1926) was an accomplished scholar, poet and music composer. He initiated shorthand and musical notations in Bengali. He wrote extensively and translated Kalidas's Meghdoot into Bengali.

Satyendranath (1842–1923) was the first Indian to join the Indian Civil Service. At the same time he was a great scholar with a large reservoir of creative talents.

Hemendranath (1844–1884) was the scientist and organiser of the family. He was a spiritual seer and Yogi of the highest order and he was responsible for development of the modern Brahmoism which is now the Adi Dharm religion. He was a "doer" of his Tagore generation and worthy successor to his grandfather Dwarkanath and father. He sided with his "conservative" siblings Dwijendranath and Birendranath in the family disputes against "modern" Satyendranath, Jyotindranath and Rabindranath.

Jyotirindranath (1849–1925) was a scholar, artist, music composer and theatre personality.

Rabindranath (1861–1941) was his youngest son. His other sons were Birendranath (1845–1915) and Somendranath.

His daughters were Soudamini, Sukumari, Saratkumari, Swarnakumari (1855–1932) and Barnakumari. Soudamini was one of the first students of Bethune School and a gifted writer. Swarnakumari was a gifted writer, editor, song-composer and social worker. All of them were famous for their beauty and education. His part in creating the legacy of Thakurbari – the House of Tagore – in the cultural heritage of Bengal, centred in Kolkata, was not negligible. It was largely through the influence of the Tagore family, following that of the writer Bankim Chandra Chatterjee, that Bengal took a leading role on the cultural front as well as on the nationalistic one, in the Renaissance in India during the nineteenth century.

As son of Dwarkanath, a close friend of Ram Mohan Roy, Debendranath came early into the influence of Brahmoism through the Brahmo Sabha, a reformist movement in Hinduism formulating as Adi Dharma (Original Dharma) what it considered as the original pristine principles of Hinduism corrupted over time.

But even earlier, deeply affected in childhood by the death of his grandmother to whom he was greatly attached, Debendranath was drawn to religion and began contemplating the meaning and nature of life. He commenced a deep study of religious literature, particularly the Upanishads. In 1839, with tutelage from Pandit Ram Chandra Vidyabageesh, a leader of the Brahmo Sabha, he formed his own active Tattwabodhini Sabha (Truthseekers' Association) to spread his new experiences and knowledge.

In 1843, Debendranath started the Tattwabodhini Patrika as mouthpiece of the Tattwabodhini Sabha. In the same year, he revived the Brahma Sabha, fallen in vigour and following since the death of Rammohun in 1833. The Brahmo Sabha was formally absorbed into the Tattwabodhini Sabha and renamed as Calcutta Brahma Samaj. The day Pous 7 of the Bengali calendar is commemorated as the foundation day of the Samaj. The Patrika became the organ of the Samaj and continued publication till 1883.

In 1848, Debendranath codified the Adi Dharma Doctrine as Brahmo Dharma Beej (Seed of the Brahmo Dharma). In 1950, he published a book titled Brahmo Dharma enshrining the fundamental principles. These principles emphasise monotheism, rationality and reject scriptural infallibility, the necessity of mediation between man and God, caste distinctions and idolatry.

With the influence of Brahmoism under Debendranath spreading far and wide throughout India, he gathered reputation as a person of particular spiritual accomplishment and came to be known as Maharshi. His spiritual stature was confirmed by Sri Ramakrishna, the great Hindu sage of the 19th century who paid Debendranath a visit . Debendranath's roles in the Indian renaissance and the reform and rejuvenation of Hindu religion are indubitable.

An influence of Hasidism over Brahmoism has been claimed.

Sivanath Sastri has paid glowing tributes to Debendranath Tagore in *History of the Brahmo Samaj*:

Maharshi Devendranath Tagore was one of the greatest religious geniuses this country ever produced. He was truly a successor of the great rishis of old. His nature was essentially spiritual. ... He was a devout follower of the Upanishadic rishis, but was no pantheist on that account. Devendranath in spite of his real sainthood never put on the grab or habits of sadhu or saint. His piety was natural, habitual and modest. He hated or shunned all display of saintliness...

He was a true and living embodiment of that teaching of the Gita where it is said: "A truly wise man is never buffeted by his trials and tribulations, does not covet pleasure, and is free from attachment, fear and anger; the same is a muni." Maharshi Devendranath was a true muni in that respect. He calmly bore all; even the greatest grieves of life. After having done his duty, he quietly rested, regardless of consequences.

Though personally not much in favour of the idea of female emancipation, he was one of the first men in Bengal to open the door of higher education to women. Valuing conscience in himself, he valued it in all about him. Religious life was growth to him; not an intellectual assent but a spiritual influence that pervaded and permeated life; consequently, he had not much sympathy with merely reformatory proceedings.

From the west he took only two ideas: first, the idea of fidelity to God; secondly the idea of public worship; in all other things he was oriental. His idea was to plant the Samaj in India, as the Hindu mode of realising universal theism, leaving the other races to realise that universal faith according to their traditional methods.

5

DWARKANATH TAGORE

Dwarkanath Tagore; (Bangla, *Darokanath Thakur*) (1794-1846), was one of the earliest entrepreneurs from India, and founder of the Jorasanko branch of the Tagore family, and is notable for making substantial contributions to the Bengal Renaissance.

Dwarkanath Tagore was the second son of Rammoni Thakur (employed in the Calcutta Police) from his first wife Menaka. Menaka was the younger sister of Alakasundari, wife to Rammoni's elder brother Ramlochan, who was childless. Soon after his birth in 1794 Dwarkanath was informally adopted by Ramlochan and Alakasundari and formally adopted in 1799.

His early education and upbringing was within the family house (*Thakur Bari*), but at age 10 in 1804 he was admitted to Sherbourne's school on the Chitpur Road and become one of Mr.Sherbourne's favourite pupils.

On 12 December 1807, Ramlochan died leaving all his property to his adopted son Dwarkanath who was then a minor. This property consisted of zamindari estates governed by the complicated Regulations of Permanent Settlement introduced by Lord Cornwallis in 1792. The zamindari being a system with harsh penalty for default and frequent auctions of defaulters, Dwarkanath left school in 1810 at the age of 16 and apprenticed himself under a renowned barrister at Calcutta Robert

Cutlar Fergusson and shuttled between Calcutta and his estates at Behrampore and Cuttack.

On 7 February 1811 Dwarkanath was married to Digambaridevi (then 9 years old and extremely goodlooking and devout). A popular myth was that she was the incarnation of the Goddess Lakshmi for Dwarkanath's family fortune took a decided turn for the better once she entered his house, also bearing him one daughter and 5 sons before her death in January 1839.

"As a zamindar Dwarkanath was mercilessly efficient and businesslike, but not generous" . Dwarkanath looked upon his investment in land as investment in any other business or enterprise and claimed what he deemed a fair return. In later years Dwarkanath would appoint European managers for his estates at Sahajadpur and Behrampore. He knew that the *ryots* were more amenable to the disciplinary control of British managers than their Bengali counterparts. In time Dwarkanath would convert his estates to integrated commercial-industrial complexes with indigo, silk and sugar factories. In the cut throat world of zamindari politics Dwarkanath took no nonsense and gave no quarter to either European or native. His knowledge of the tenancy laws stood him in good stead. Unlike his good friend Rammohun Roy who pleaded for the rights of the poor ryots, Dwarkanath's sympathies were more one sided and tilted towards his own class.

In 1822 Dwarkanath, while carrying on his private ventures, took additional service in the British East India Company as *Shestidar* to Trevor Plowden Collector for the 24-Parganas. Although the pay was meagre at under Rs.500 per year, the prestige and avenues for additional income was considerable and gave Dwarkanath an intimate insight into the functioning of the government. Trevor Plowden formed a lifelong friendship with Dwarkanath. In 1827 there arose a great scandal in the Salt Revenue department centred on a dishonest Dewan, and assured of Dwarkanath's own personal integrity and character, he was requested to take over as Dewan of the Board. He did not take long to rend asunder the network of corruption which resulted in a counter petition against him to the Board accusing him of defalcation. To clear his name an enquiry was ordered which at each stage of enquiry, by the Board, by the Governor General and finally by the India Office at London cleared him unreservedly. By then Dwarkanath had had enough of Government service and resigned in June 1834 to launch into his spectacular career as a full time entrepreneur.

Dwarkanath Tagore was of the firm conviction that at those times "the happiness of India is best secured by her connection with England". Dwarkanath was no doubt a loyalist, and a sincere one at that, but he was by no means a toady. Servility was as far from his character as was lack of generosity from his nature. He was also firm in defending the interest and sentiments of his people against European prejudices. With this in view he established on 21 March 1838 an Association for Landholders (later known as the Landholder's Society). The association was overtly a self serving political association, founded on a large and liberal basis, to admit landholders of all descriptions, Englishmen,Hindus Mussalman and Christian. What is interesting is that cut across racial and religious divides being founded along with his old rival Raja Radhakant Deb with whom he had earlier founded the Gaudiya Sabha. It was the first political association in India to ventilate in a constitutional manner the grievances of the people or a section of them that were outspoken. From this grew the British India Association, the precursor to the Indian National Congress.

Dwarkanath Tagore died on the evening of Saturday 1 August 1846 at the St. George's Hotel in London during a tremendous thunderstorm the likes of which had not been seen for many years past. He was buried at Kensal Green on 5 August 1846 in a private ceremony without any religious observances. His heart which had been previously extracted was sent to Calcutta to conduct the Brahmo rites amidst great controversy. In his obituary *The London Mail* of 7 August wrote *"Descended from the highest Brahmin caste of India his family can prove a long and undoubted pedigree. But it is not on account of this nobility that we review his life but on far better grounds. .. However gifted, his claims rest on a higher pedestal - he was the benefactor of the country. .. They testified to his merits in the encouragement of every public and private undertaking likely to benefit India."*

Dwarkanath was a western-educated Bengali brahmin and an acknowledged civic leader of Kolkata who played a pioneering role in setting up a string of commercial ventures — banking, insurance and shipping companies — in partnership with British traders. He is the architect of the first bi-racial agency house from India, Carr, Tagore and Company (even earlier, Rustomjee Cowasjee, a Parsi in Calcutta, had formed an inter-racial firm but in the early 19th century, Parsis were classified as a Near Eastern community as opposed to South Asian). Tagore's company managed huge zamindary estates spread across today's West Bengal and Orissa states in India, and in Bangladesh, besides holding large stakes in new enterprises that were tapping the rich coal seams of Bengal, running tug services between Calcutta and the mouth of the river Hooghly and transplanting Chinese tea crop to the plains of Upper Assam. This company was one of those Indian private companies engaged in the Opium Trade with China. Production of opium was in India and it was sold in China. When the Chinese protested, the East India company shifted the business to the proxy of certain selected Indian companies of which this was one. Very large schooners were engaged in shipments. This made Dwarkanath extremely rich. And there are legends about the extent of it.

A restless soul, with a firm conviction that his racial identity was not a barrier between him and other Britons as long as he remained loyal to the British Sovereign, Tagore was well-received by Queen Victoria and many other British and European notables during his two trips to the West in the 1840s; he died in London after a brief illness. Historiographers have often been flummoxed by his inability, despite a great desire, to be honoured by the Queen with a baronetcy (his grandson,

Rabindranath, received the honour but returned it following British atrocities at the Jallianwala Bagh in the Punjab, 1919).

Some scholars have been puzzled by the paucity of documents concerning Dwarkanath in the Tagore family collections spread over many generations. There are scanty references to him in the records of Debendranath Tagore, his eldest son who founded the Brahmo religion. There is absolutely no mention of Dwarkanath (except in a personal letter) in the monumental body of writings by his grandson Rabindranath. The established academic view is that Dwarkanath's concept of equating the coloniser with the colonised was found galling by his countrymen in the context of the nationalist awakening in Bengal and India, in the latter half of the nineteenth century, of which the Brahmo movement initiated was an integral part. The first Indian entrepreneur who thought globally thus remains an oddity in the country's socio-cultural history.

6

BENGAL RENAISSANCE

The Bengal Renaissance refers to a social reform movement during the nineteenth and early twentieth centuries in the region of Bengal during the period of British rule. The Bengal renaissance can be said to have started with Raja Ram Mohan Roy (1775-1833) and ended with Rabindranath Tagore (1861-1941), although there have been many stalwarts thereafter embodying particular aspects of the unique intellectual and creative output. Nineteenth century Bengal was a unique blend of religious and social reformers, scholars, literary giants, journalists, patriotic orators and scientists, all merging to form the image of a renaissance, and marked the transition from the 'medieval' to the 'modern' .

During this period, Bengal witnessed an intellectual awakening that is in some way similar to the Renaissance in Europe during the 16th century, although Europeans of that age were not confronted with the challenge and influence of alien colonialism. This movement questioned existing orthodoxies, particularly with respect to women, marriage, the dowry system, the caste system, and religion. One of the earliest social movements that emerged during this time was the Young Bengal movement, that espoused rationalism and atheism as the common denominators of civil conduct among upper caste educated Hindus.

The parallel socio-religious movement, the Brahmo Samaj, developed during this time period and counted many of the leaders of the Bengal Renaissance among its followers . In the earlier years the Brahmo Samaj, like the rest of society, could not however, conceptualize, in that feudal-colonial era, a free India as it was influenced by the European Enlightenment (and its bearers in India, the British Raj) although it traced its intellectual roots to the Upanishads. Their version of Hinduism, or rather Universal Religion (similar to that of Ramakrishna), although devoid of practices like sati and polygamy that had crept into the social aspects of Hindu life, was ultimately a rigid impersonal monotheistic faith, which actually was quite distinct from the pluralistic and multifaceted nature of the way the Hindu religion was practiced. Future leaders like Keshub Chunder Sen were as much devotees of Christ, as they were of Brahma, Krishna or the Buddha. It has been argued by some scholars that the Brahmo Samaj movement never gained the support of the masses and remained restricted to the elite, although Hindu society has accepted most of the social reform programmes of the Brahmo Samaj. It must also be acknowledged that many of the later Brahmos were also leaders of the freedom movement.

The renaissance period after the Indian Rebellion of 1857 saw a magnificent outburst of Bengali literature. While Ram Mohan Roy and Iswar Chandra Vidyasagar were the pioneers, others like Bankim Chandra Chatterjee widened it and built upon it . The first significant nationalist detour to the Bengal Renaissance was given by the brilliant writings of Bankim Chandra Chatterjee. Later writers of the period who introduced broad discussion of social problems and more colloquial forms of Bengali into mainstream literature included the great Saratchandra Chatterjee.

The Tagore family, including Rabindranath Tagore, were leaders of this period and had a particular interest in educational reform . Their contribution to the Bengal Renaissance was multi-faceted. Indeed, Tagore's 1901 Bengali novella, *Nastanirh* was written as a critique of men who professed to follow the ideals of the Renaissance, but failed to do so within their own families. In many ways Rabindranath Tagore's writings (especially poems and songs) can be seen as imbued with the spirit of the Upanishads. His works repeatedly allude to Upanishadic ideas regarding soul, liberation, transmigration and — perhaps most essentially — about a spirit that imbues all creation not unlike the Upanishadic Brahman. Tagore's English translation of a set of poems titled the Gitanjali won him the Nobel Prize for Literature in 1913. He was the first Asian to win this award. That was the only example at the time but the contribution of the Tagore family is enormous.

The word "renaissance" in European history meant "rebirth" and was used in the context of the revival of the Graeco-Roman learning in the fifteenth and sixteenth centuries after the long winter of the dark medieval period. A serious comparison was started by the dramatis personae of the Bengal renaissance like Keshub Chunder Sen, Bipin Chandra Pal and M. N. Roy. For about a century, Bengal's conscious awareness and the changing modern world was more developed and ahead of the rest of India. The role played by Bengal in the modern awakening of India is thus comparable to the position occupied by Italy in the European renaissance. Very much like the Italian Renaissance, it was not a mass movement; but instead restricted to the upper classes. Though the Bengal Renaissance was the "culmination of the process of emergence of the cultural characteristics of the Bengali people that had started in the age of Hussein Shah, it remained predominantly Hindu and only partially Muslim. Swami Vivekananda who founded Ramakrishna Mission is considered a key figure in the introduction of Hindu philosophies of Vedanta and Yoga in Europe and America, and is also credited with rising interfaith awareness, bringing Hinduism to the status of a world religion during the end of the 19th century. Vivekananda is considered to be a major force in the revival of Hinduism in modern India. He is best known for his inspiring speech beginning with "sisters and brothers of America", through which he introduced Hinduism at the Parliament of the World's Religions at Chicago in 1893.

Several leaders of 20th Century India and philosophers have acknowledged Vivekananda's influence. The first governor general of independent India, Chakravarti Rajagopalachari, once observed that "Vivekananda saved Hinduism, saved India." According to Subhas Chandra Bose, Vivekananda "is the maker of modern India" and for Mohandas Gandhi, Vivekananda's influence increased his "love for his country a thousandfold." National Youth Day in India is held on his birthday, January 12, to commemorate him. This was a most fitting gesture as much of Swami Vivekananda's writings concerned the Indian youth and how they should strive to uphold their ancient values whilst fully participating in the modern world.

"

During nineteenth century A.D., Bengal produced a galaxy of reform movements among the Hindus which had also given birth to the contemporary Hindu reform movements such as Brahmo Samaj and Arya Samaj, which thrived in Bengal side by side with them... Raja Ram Mohan Roy's movement is generally regarded as 'Renaissance movement'. It is called by some as Hindu Renaissance and by others as Bengali Renaissance movement. It should nevertheless be observed that compared with the European 'Renaissance model', it was a Renaissance with a difference, especially, deeply inlaid by a revivalist make-up of pristine Hindu or Aryan religious spirit... Raja Ram Mohan Roy's Renaissance aimed at resuscitating the pristine Aryan spirit, 'Unitarianism of God', with the help of modern Western rationalist spirit.

During the Bengal Renaissance science was also advanced by several Bengali scientists such as Satyendra Nath Bose and Jagadish Chandra Bose. Sir Jagadish Chandra Bose was a polymath: a physicist, biologist, botanist, archaeologist, and writer of science fiction. He pioneered the investigation of radio and microwave optics, made very significant contributions to plant science, and laid the foundations of experimental science in the Indian subcontinent. He is considered one of the fathers of radio science, and is also considered the father of

Bengali science fiction. He was the first from the Indian subcontinent to get a US patent, in 1904.

Satyendra Nath Bose was a physicist, specializing in mathematical physics. He is best known for his work on quantum mechanics in the early 1920s, providing the foundation for Bose-Einstein statistics and the theory of the Bose-Einstein condensate. He is honoured as the namesake of the boson. Although more than one Nobel Prize was awarded for research related to the concepts of the boson, Bose-Einstein statistics and Bose-Einstein condensate—the latest being the 2001 Nobel Prize in Physics, which was given for advancing the theory of Bose-Einstein condensates—Bose himself was never awarded the Nobel Prize.

According to historian Romesh Chunder Dutt:

"The conquest of Bengal by the English was not only a political revolution, but ushered in a greater revolution in thoughts and ideas, in religion and society... From the stories of gods and goddesses, kings and queens, princes and princesses, we have learnt to descend to the humble walks of life, to sympathise with the common citizen or even common peasant ... Every revolution is attended with vigour, and the present one is no exception to the rule. Nowhere in the annals of Bengali literature are so many and so bright names found crowded together in the limited space of one century as those of Ram Mohan Roy, Akshay Kumar Datta, Ishwar Chandra Vidyasagar, Michael Madhusudan Dutt, Hem Chandra Banerjee, Bankim Chandra Chatterjee and Dina Bandhu Mitra. Within the three quarters of the present century, prose, blank verse, historical fiction and drama have been introduced for the first time in the Bengali literature...

7

TAGORE FAMILY

The Tagore family, with over three hundred years of history, has been one of the leading families of Kolkata, and is regarded as a key influence during the Bengal Renaissance. The family has produced several persons who have contributed substantially in the fields of business, social and religious reformation, literature, art and music.

"Europeans" started coming to Bengal in the 17th century. After the Battle of Plassey, the British became the ruling power.

The Bengal renaissance of the 19th century was a remarkable period of societal transformation in which whole range of creative activities – literary, cultural, social and economic- flourished The Bengal Renaissance was the culmination of the process of emergence of the cultural characteristics of the Bengali people that had started in the age of Hussein Shah (1493–1519). This spread over covering around three centuries had a tremendous impact on Bengali society. Incidentally that coincided with the rise of the Tagore family. The Tagore family attained prominence during this period through its unusual social positioning between Indian and European influences.

To quote Chitra Deb, "Though the cultural role of the Thakurs has received the greatest attention by far, their importance on final assessment is a composite one: commercial and political as well as literary and musical. They played a collective role in every patriotic movement of their times: Nabagopal Mitra's Hindu Mela, the Congress and the National

Conference, the Rakhi Festival of 1905, and the Nationalist Movement generally. The story of the Thakurs is inseparable from the story of Calcutta, Bengal and India."

The family earlier held the title (surname) of Kushari, and hailed from Jessore District, now in Bangladesh. Two of the Kusharis, Panchanan and Sukdeb, settled in Gobindapur, one of the villages that developed into the city of Kolkata, and engaged in stevedoring business. Being Brahmins, the neighbours called them *Thakurmashai*, or 'holy sir'. After the British gained control of the country, 'Thakur' became their family name. In English, it was Anglicized to 'Tagore', with some variations in spelling within the family. They were Pirali Brahmins, a sort of outcaste in orthodox Hindu society due to their conversions to Islam.

Darpanarayan Tagore (1731-1791), the first person in the family to gain prominence, earned major revenues through money-lending while spent as abundantly as he earned. When he quarrelled with his brother Nilmani Tagore over family matters the latter shifted out of the family household and settled in Mechuabazar, which later came to be known as Jorasanko. Subsequently, several other branches of the family settled in Pathuriaghata, Kailahata and Chorbagan, all neighbourhoods of the fledgling metropolis, particularly when Gobindapur was razed by the British for the construction of the new Fort William.

Gopimohan Tagore (1760–1819) was well known for his wealth and in 1822, made what may be the largest ever gift of gold to the Kali temple at Kalighat. He was one of the founders of Hindu College, the institution that initiated western education in the country. He knew English, French, Portuguese, Sanskrit, Persian and Urdu, apart from Bengali.

Prasanna Coomar Tagore, (1801–1868), son of Gopimohan Tagore, was one of the leaders of the Landholders' Society and later the president of the British Indian Association, the earliest organisations of Indians in the country. He had started as government lawyer but later turned his attention to family matters. Apart from being a director of Hindu College, he was involved with the activities of several institutions. Tagore Law lectures are organised by Calcutta University on the strength of donations he made. He was founder of the first local theatre – the Hindu theatre. He was the first Indian to be appointed to the Viceregal Legislative Council.

Gnanendramohan Tagore (1826–1890), son of Prasanna Coomar Tagore, converted to Christianity and married Kamalmani daughter of Krishna Mohan Banerjee. He was disowned by his father and disinherited. He went to England and qualified for the bar from Lincoln's Inn. He became the first Indian to become a barrister. For sometime he taught Hindu Law and Bengali at the University of London.

Jatindramohan Tagore (1831–1908), son of Harakumar Tagore, inherited the Pathuriaghata branch wealth. He contributed substantially to the development of theatre in Kolkata and was himself a keen actor. He inspired Michael Madhusudan Dutt to write *Tilottamasambhab Kabya* and published it at his cost. In 1865, he established the Banganatyalaya at Pathuriaghata. He was keen in music also and patronised musicians. With his active support one of them, Kshetra Mohan Goswami, introduced the concept of orchestra in to Indian music for the first time in this country. He was president of the British Indian Association and was the first Indian to be member of the Royal Photographic Society.

Ramanath Tagore (1801–1877) and Jatindramohan were major patrons of European art. Their palatial home, the Tagore Castle at Pathuriaghta had a major collection of European painters. Subsequently, members of the family took to oil-painting. Shoutindramohan Tagore (1865–98) was one of the first Indians to have studied at the Royal Academy.

Shourindramohan Tagore (180-1914), son of Harakumar Tagore, was a great musician who was awarded the doctor of music titles by Philadelphia University in 1875 and by Oxford University in 1896. He was proficient in both Indian and Western music. He founded the Banga Sangeet Vidyalaya in 1871 and the Bengal Academy of Music in 1881. He was honoured by the Shah of Iran with the 'Nabab Shahzada' title. The British government made him 'Knight Bachelor of the United Kingdom'. He was also a playwright and Justice of the Peace. He was also a leading philanthropist of his time.

Dwarkanath Tagore (1794–1846) was the man who ushered the family into its special role in Bengali history and culture. He was son of Nilmani Tagore's second son, Rammani Tagore, but was adopted by the childless elder son, Ramlochan Tagore. He not only inherited the great wealth of the Jorasanko family but also built up an extensive business empire even while he worked as *sheristadar*, the highest position then open to Indians. He was a luxury loving prodigal. His manners led his European friends to call him 'Prince'. He was a friend of Raja Rammohun Roy and played a leading role in the social development of the country. He was a shareholder of Macintosh & Co, a director of the Commercial Bank, founder of the Union Bank, director of several insurance companies, established Carr & Tagore Co. and engaged in coal mining (pioneering work), silk and indigo trade, shipping and sugar manufacture. He established himself as an industrialist and one of the leading rich men in the society of his time.

He was the second person amongst the educated Indians, after Raja Rammohun Roy to sail to England in 1842, with two persons accompanying him, ignoring the prohibition of the pandits. Rabindranath Tagore's creative multiplicity or Debendranath Tagore's spiritual pursuits were, to a considerable extent, made possible because of the foundations of leisure provided by Dwarakanath Tagore's wealth.

After Dwarkanath Tagore, the leadership of the family passed on to Debendranath Tagore(1807–1905) and Girindranath Tagore, the two sons of Dwarkanath Tagore. Debendranath Tagore founded the Brahmo religion and also started its journal Tattwabodhini Patrika. His children continued in the Brahmo Samaj. Girindranath Tagore also joined the Brahmo Samaj but his children, Ganendra and Gunendra, did not. Gunendra's sons, Gaganendra, Samarendra and Abanindra branched out but retained cordial relationship with the Jorasanko family. Debendranath Tagore took over the reins of the Brahmo Samaj in 1843 and not only resurrected it but also enriched it in many ways. It became the inspirtaion for the Bengal Renaissance. It was he who gave the Brahmo movement the trappings of a separate faith and introduced its own unique rituals. The Brahmo Samaj cast a very wide-ranging influence on its parent Hindu society, much wider than its limited membership would ostensibly permit.

Several of Debendranath Tagore's children were brilliant. Dwijendranath Tagore (1840–1926) was a great scholar, poet and music composer. He wrote extensively in the newspapers and magazines of the day on literature, philosophy and religion. He was editor of "Bharati" and Tattwabodhini Patrika. A pioneer in Bengali shorthand, he was one of organisers of the Hindu Mela

Satyendranath Tagore, (1842–1923), was the first Indian to join the Indian Civil Service.in 1864. Earlier, he and his brother Ganendranath were among the first students to pass the Entrance Examination of Calcutta University in 1857. Even while serving in an adminsistrative job, he was a prolific writer, poet and song composer. Many of his nationalist songs are still sung. He was editor of "Tattwabodhini Patrika" and took an active interest in the Hindu Mela. He encourage his wife, Gyanadanandini Debi, to adopt western ideas and for that purpose took her to a governor's party and also to England, something unthinkable in those days.

Debendranath's third son Hemendranath was a strict disciplinarian who was entrusted with the responsibility of looking after the education of his younger brothers as well as administrating the large family estates.Like most of Debendranath's children, he had varied interests in different fields.On one hand he composed a number of "Bromhosangeets" and on the other,wrote articles on physical science which he planned to compile and edit into a text book for school students.If his untimely death had not prevented him from completing the project,this would certainly have been the first science text book to be written in Bengali.He was known for his physical strength and wrestling skills. Exceptionally for the times,he insisted on a formal education for his daughters.He not only put them through school but trained them in music, arts and European languages such as French and German.It was another mark of his forward looking mentality that he actively sought out eligible grooms from different provinces of India for his daughters and married them off in places as far away as UP and Assam.

Jyotirindranath Tagore (1849–1925) was a scholar, artist, music composer and theatre personality. He knew several languages – Bengali, Sanskrit, English, Bengali, Marathi and Persian. In 1924, he translated "Gita Rahasya" of Bal Gangadhar Tilak into Bengali. He also translated several other books. He wrote several plays, and directed and acted in them. He composed songs that are still available in CDs. Around 2,000 of his paintings are in possession of Rabindra Bharati. A selection of his paintings were published in London in 1914, at the instance of Rothenstein.

Rabindranath Tagore (1861–1941) his youngest son, was the first Asian to win a Nobel Prize, and was exceptionally talented and the most famous in the family. Rabindrinath is best remembered in history for writing what became the national anthems of the nations of India and Bangladesh and for coining the title Mahatma for Indian nationalist leader Mohandas Gandhi

Amongst his daughters Swarnakumari Devi (1855–1932) was a gifted writer, editor, song-composer and social worker. She was editor of "Bharati", a remarkabale performance in an age when very few girls went to school. She also edited a children's magazine Balak. Sakhi Samiti was developed by her as means for upliftment of women. Her husband Janakinath Ghosal was one of the founders of the Indian National Congress. As a result she also participated in his nationalistic activities. She was the author of several books.

The Artists

After Rabindranath, the most notable in the Jorasanko family were Gaganendranath Tagore (1867–1938), Abanindranath Tagore (1871–1951), and Sunayani (1875–1962). They made an immense contribution to Indian art. Even earlier, Abanindranath Tagore's grand father and father, Gindranath (1820–1854), Gunendranath (1847–81), and subsequently Abaindranath Tagore's cousin, Hitendranath Tagore (1867–1908) and his nephew Jaminiprakash Ganguli, were all gifted and prolific painters, specialising in a genre of dusky landscapes and romantic studies of peasant life.

Gaganendranath was a pioneer in many ways – in adopting Indian styles of painting after training in western art, and then absorbing Japanese styles. However, it was his brother Abanindranath who inaugurated what became known as the "Bengal school" or "Neo-Oriental school". Its influence spread across the country while it incorporated various strains of South Asian influence.

The Younger Generation

The younger generation also contributed substantially. Dwijendranath's second son Sudhindranath (1869–1929) was a renowned author. His son Soumyendranath (1901–74) was well-known as a leftist politician. Satyendranath's son Surendranath (1872–1940) also had political links. His daughter Indira (1873–1960) distinguished herself in literature, music and women's movement. She married Pramatha Chowdhury, a distinguished scholar and writer. The list does not end here. All of them had enormous talent and were brought up in an ideal environment of literary debates and discussions, musical compositions, painting, and theatrical performances. Sharmila Tagore, a well-known Mumbai actress, connected with Tagore on both sides, in an interview stated that her mother's mother, Latika Tagore was the grand daughter of Rabindranath Tagore's brother, Hijendranath .

The environment at Jorasanko was filled with literature, music, painting and theatre. They had their own education system. In the earlier days, the women did not go to school but they were all educated at home. Swarnakumari Debi has recalled how in her early days the governess would write something on a slate which the girls then had to copy. When Debedranath discovered this, he at once stopped such a mindless and mechanical method and brought in a better teacher, Ajodhyanath Pakrashi – a male outsider in the women's quarters... Some of the sons like Ganendra, Gunendra and Jyoitrindra set up their own private theatre. To start with men played in the role of women, but over a period of time even the women joined. The environment in the family played a major role in the development of its members. Even Rabindranath Tagore who went to win the Nobel Prize in literature had very little formal education.

Being somewhat conservative, Debendranath Tagore had put in many restrictions about members of the family participating in certain types of activities outside the house. Therefore, they brought the outside world into their house and the entire family, including the women participated. Two small examples will illustrate the environment:

"A baiji named Saraswatibai, renowned for her singing, had come from Kashi. We wanted to listen to her singing. She charged six hundred rupees for a single night's performance. We sent Shyamsundar, "Go and bargain, see what you can manage." Shyamsundar went and could fix her up for three hundred rupees. He came back and said, "Three hundred rupees and two bottles of brandy." On hearing about the brandy we were taken aback, mummy could object. Shyamsundar said, "She cannot sing without taking brandy." Everything was ready. Saraswati entered the gathering. She was demure, round nosed, nothing great. Natore said, "Abanda, what have you done? Just thrown away three hundred rupees." She was going to sing two songs. Natore was ready to accompany her on the mridangam. As the clock struck ten she started singing.

One song and it was eleven at night. Natore was paralysed with the mridnagam in his laps. The wonderful voice of Saraswati reverberated around that dance-hall. How wonderfully she had tuned her voice. Some of us with pillows in our laps, others with hands close to our hearts, we were all wonderstruck. The gathering was won over with just one song. Everyone was still immersed in the song, when Saraswati said, "Aur kuch farmaiye." (present your wish). After listening to her, no one dared to put anything forward. Then I told Shyamsundar, "Ask her to sing a bhajan. We have heard that bhajans of Kashi are very famous." She sang a bhajan known to all, "Ao to Brajachandalal..." (Come oh, Lord!) Everybody was dumb-founded...

"... The atarwala (scent seller) had come, we used to call him Gabriel Saheb, a genuine Jew. It was as if Shylock from Shakespeare's *Merchant of Venice* had come alive and travelled all the way from Istambul to sell atar (scent) on the southern veranda of the Jorasanko house... so many types of people came and so much happened..."

Although the Jorasanko branch of the family had close links with Shilaidaha, in Kushtia District, now in Bangladesh and Santiniketan, where Rabindranath developed Viswa Bharati, their roots were in the Jorasanko house. It was popular as Jorasanko Thakur Bari of the Tagores and now houses the Rabindra Bharati University.

8

BRAHMO SAMAJ

Brahmo Samaj is the societal component of the Brahmo religion which is mainly practiced today as the Adi Dharm after its eclipse in Bengal consequent to the exit of the Tattwabodini Sabha from its ranks in 1859. It was one of the most influential religious movements responsible for the making of modern India. It was conceived at Kolkata in 1830 by Dwarkanath Tagore and Ram Mohan Roy as reformation of the prevailing Brahmanism of the time (specifically Kulin practices) and began the Bengal Renaissance of the 19th century pioneering all religious, social and educational advance of the Hindu community in the 19th century. From the *Brahmo Samaj* springs Brahmoism, the most recent of India's faiths recognised in law as distinct religions and Bangladesh , reflecting its non-syncretic "foundation of Rammohun Roy's reformed spiritual Hinduism (contained in the 1830 Banian deed) and inclusion of root Hebraic - Islamic creed and practice." After the publication of Hemendranath Tagore's Brahmo *Anusthan* (code of practice) in 1860 which formally divorced Brahmoism from Hinduism, the first Brahmo Samaj was founded in 1861 at Lahore by Pandit Nobin Chandra Roy.

On 20 August 1828 the first assembly of the *Brahmo Sabha* (progenitor of the Brahmo Samaj) was held at the North Calcutta house of *Feringhee* Kamal Bose. This day is celebrated by Brahmos as *Bhadrotsab* [*Bhadrotshôb* "Bhadro celebration"). This *Sabha* was convened at Calcutta by religious reformer Raja

Rammohun Roy for his family and friends settled there. The *Sabha* regularly gathered on Saturday between seven o'clock to nine o'clock. These were informal meetings of Bengali Brahmins (the "twice born"), accompanied by Upanishadic recitations in Sanskrit followed by Bengali translations of the Sanskrit recitation and singing of Brahmo hymns composed by Rammohun. These meetings were open to all Brahmins and there was no formal organisation or theology as such.

On 8 January 1830 influential progressive members of the closely related Kulin Brahmin clan (scurrilously described as Pirali Brahmin *ie.* ostracised for service in the Mughal *Nizaamat* of Bengal) of Tagore (*Thakur*) and Roy (*Vandopadhyaya*) *zumeendar* family mutually executed the Trust deed of Brahmo Sabha for the first Adi Brahmo Samaj (place of worship) on Chitpore Road (now Rabindra Sarani), Kolkata, India with Ram Chandra Vidyabagish as first resident superintendent.

On 23 January 1830 or 11th *Magh*, the *Adi Brahmo* premises were publicly inaugurated (with about 500 Brahmins and 1 Englishman present). This day is celebrated by Brahmos as *Maghotsab* (*Maghotshôb* "Magh celebration").

In November 1830 Rammohun Roy left for England.

With Rammohun's departure for England in 1830, the affairs of Brahmo Sabha were effectively managed by Trustees Dwarkanath Tagore and Pandit Ram Chandra Vidyabagish, with Dwarkanath instructing his *diwan* to manage affairs. Weekly service were held consonant with the Trust directive, consisting of three successive parts: recitation of the Vedas by Telegu Brahmins in the closed apartment exclusively before the Brahmin members of the congregation, reading and exposition of the Upanishads for the general audience, and singing of religious hymns. The reading of the Vedas was done exclusively before the Brahmin participants as the orthodox Telugu Brahmin community and its members could not be persuaded to recite the Vedas before Brahmins and non-Brahmins alike.

By the time of Rammohun's death in 1833 near Bristol (UK), attendance at the *Sabha* dwindled and the Telugu Brahmins revived idolatry. The *zumeendars,* being preoccupied in business, had little time for affairs of *Sabha,* and flame of *Sabha* was almost extinguished.

Tattwabodhini Period

On 6 October 1839 Debendranath Tagore, son of (Prince) Dwarkanath Tagore, established *Tattvaranjini Sabha* which was shortly thereafter renamed the Tattwabodhini (*Truth-seekers*) Sabha. Initially confined to immediate members of the Tagore family, in 2 years it mustered over 500 members. In 1840 Debendranath published a Bangla translation of *Katha Upanishad.* A modern researcher describes the Sabha's philosophy as *modern middle-class (bourgeois) Vedanta.* Among its first members were the "two giants of Hindu reformation and Bengal Renaissance, Akshay Kumar Datta "who in 1839 emerged from the life of an anonymous squalor-beset individual" and Ishwar Chandra Vidyasagar the "indigenous modernizer".

On 7th Pous 1765 Shaka (1843) Debendranath Tagore and twenty other Tattwabodhini stalwarts were formally invited by Pt. Vidyabagish into the Trust of Brahmo Sabha. The Pous Mela at Santiniketan starts on this day . From this day forth, the Tattwabodhini Sabha dedicated itself to promoting Ram Mohan Roy's creed. The other Brahmins who swore the First Covenant of Brahmoism are:-

Shridhar Bhattacharya
Shyamacharan Bhattacharya
Brajendranath Tagore
Girindranath Tagore, brother of Debendranath Tagore & father of Ganendranath Tagore
Anandachandra Bhattacharya
Taraknath Bhattacharya
Haradev Chattopadhyaya, the future father-in-law to MahaAcharya Hemendranath Tagore
Shyamacharan Mukhopadhyaya
Ramnarayan Chattopadhyaya
Sashibhushan Mukhopadhyaya

In Nov 1855 the Rev. Charles Dall (a Unitarian minister of Boston) arrived in Calcutta to start his mission and immediately established contact with Debendranath and other Brahmos. Debendranath's suspicion of foreigners alienated Dall and in 1857, Debendranath Tagore barred the entry of the Reverend from the Sabha premises for preaching *the name of Christ who some people worship as God* within. Debendranath then proceeded on spiritual retreat to Simla. Dall, immediately formed a counter group "The friends of Rammmohun Roy Society" and then got admitted a protege to Sabha. The presence of Dall's protege Keshub Chandra Sen (a non-Brahmin) into the Calcutta Brahmo Sabha in 1857 while Debendranath was away in Simla caused considerable stress in the movement, with many long time Tattvabodhini Brahmin members publicly leaving the Brahmo Sabha and institutions due to his high-handed ways. In September 1858, Debendranath returned to Calcutta to resolve the simmering disputes. but his conservative mien did not allow him to take decisive steps. He proceeded on a sea voyage to Ceylon accompanied by Sen and his 2nd son Satyendranath (a firm admirer of Mr Sen) but no concord was achieved. In 1859, the venerable and beloved Secretary of the Tattwabodhini Sabha Ishwar Chandra Vidyasagar resigned from the Brahmo Sabha in the face of Debendranath's vacillation. A meeting of the Tatwabodhini was promptly summoned with Debendranath resigning from the group he had founded. His third son Hemendranath Tagore then a boy barely 15 years in age, and the favorite pupil of Vidyasgar, was commonly acclaimed as Debendranath's successor to head the Tattwabodhini. In the course of time he would become known as the *MahaAcharya* (or *Great Teacher*).

Disgusted by politics within the Tagore family and the support to K.C.Sen's faction by his own brother Satyendranath Tagore, Hemendranath took the bold decisions to expand his Sabha out from Calcutta. His close associate Pandit Nobin Chandra Roy who had joined the new institution of "Railways" in 1860 as its "Paymaster" for Upper India was tasked to spread Brahmoism there. With a predominantly monotheistic populace following Islam and Sikhism it was perceived as fertile soil for Rammohun's message. The Tattwabodhini decreed that the uncorrupted faith of the original 1830 Trust Deed would be known there as the Adi Dharm to distinguish it from the distorted versions of the squabbling factions of Calcutta. The steps taken by Hemendranath Tagore, with the blessing of his father, was to institute in 1860 a suit before the Supreme Court to restore the title "Brahmo Samaj" to his faction. After losing in this suit in 1861, Keshub Sen's faction altered the name of their Samaj from "The Brahmo Samaj of India" to "Navabidhan (or the New Dispensation)". With victory in this suit and the promulgation of his *Brahmo Anusthan* (Code of Brahmaic doctrine and practice) in 1861, Hemendranath's Samaj-ists are henceforth known as the "Anusthanic" Brahmos (or Brahmos who follow the Code). The other factions were designated as "*An*anusthanic" Brahmos (or those who do not follow the Code) (this distinction was again to be legally examined before the Privy Council of Great Britain in 1901 and in 1902 the Privy Council upheld the 1897 finding of the Chief Court of the Punjab that the Adi Dharm (*anusthanic* Brahmos) were definitely not Hindus whereas the *Ananusthanics* Brahmos of Calcutta fall within Hinduism).

Controversies over foundation of Brahmo Samaj ?

Who founded the Brahmo Samaj ?

The Brahmo Samaj was founded at Lahore in 1861 by Pandit Navin Chandra Roy to propagate the Brahmo religion. Nobin Chunder Roy had been deputed by MahaAcharya Hemendranath Tagore to spread the new Adi Dharma message of casteless Vedic Aryanism in Upper India and rescue Christian converts to the fold of the national religion.

Who founded the Brahmo religion ?

The Brahmo religion was founded in 1849 at Calcutta by Debendranath Tagore with the publication of "Brahmo Dharma". This work established Brahmoism as a separate religion apart from all others.

Is not Raja Ram Mohan Roy the Brahmo Samaj founder ?

Ram Mohan Roy started the Brahma Sabha (Association of Brahmins) along with Dwarkanath Tagore in 1828. The objectives of this association were to publicize the true Vedanta which had been corrupted by Buddhist and Brahmanical influences. The Sabha met every Wednesday at Kamal Basu's house in Chitpur and later moved to their own premises at Chitpur Road in 1830 (purchased by the munificence Dwarkanath Tagore) . After the death of Ram Mohan Roy in 1833, the Sabha became moribund.

Are these Chitpur premises of 1830 not the Adi Brahmo Samaj?

It is correct that the present Adi Brahmo Samaj premises are situated at the same location as 1830. However, the Adi Brahmo Samaj is only the name given by the common people to the Calcutta Bramho Samaj when Keshub Chunder Sen and a few of his sympathisers were expelled from it by MahaAcharya.

If the Calcutta Brahmo Samaj is the same as Adi Brahmo Samaj, when was it founded ?

The Calcutta Brahmo Samaj was so named in 1863, when after a cyclone the Chitpur Road premises were affected and Brahma Sabha (previously amalgamated with Tattwabodhini Sabha) was shifted to the Jorasako Thakur bari.

First Secession

Disagreement with the Tattvabodhini came to a head publicly between the period of 1 August 1865 till November 1866 with many tiny splinter groups styling themselves as *Brahmo*. The most notable of these groups styled itself "Brahmo Samaj of India". This period is also referred to in the histories of the secessionists as the "First Schism".

Current status and number of adherents

While the various Calcutta sponsored movements declined after 1920 and faded into obscurity after the Partition of India, the Adi Dharm creed has expanded and is now the 9th largest of India's enumerated religions with 7.83 million adherents, heavily concentrated between the states of Punjab and Uttar Pradesh. In the Indian census of 2001 only 177 persons declared themselves a "Brahmo", but the number of subscriber members to Brahmo Samaj is somewhat larger at around 20,000 members.

In all fields of social reform, including abolition of the caste system and of the dowry system, emancipation of women, and improving the educational system, the *Brahmo Samaj* reflected the ideologies of the Bengal Renaissance. Brahmoism, as a means of discussing the dowry system, was a central theme of Sarat Chandra Chattopadhyay's noted 1914 Bengali language novella, *Parineeta*.

After controversies, including the controversy over Keshub Chunder Sen's daughter's child marriage rituals wherein the validity of Brahmo marriages were questioned and split the *Brahmo Samaj of India*, the *Brahmo Samaj Marriage Bill of 1871* was enacted as the *Special Marriages Act of 1872* and set the age at which girls could be married at 14. All Brahmo marriages were thereafter solemnised under this law which required the affirmation "I am not Hindu, nor a Mussalman, nor a Christian". The Special Marriages Act 1872 was repealed by the new Special Marriages Act in 1954 which became the secular Marriage law for India. The old Special Marriages Act of 1872 was allowed to live on as the Hindu Marriage Act 1955 for Hindus - Brahmo Religionists are excluded from this Act; which is applicable, however, to Hindus who follow the Brahmo Samaj. On May 5, 2004 the Supreme Court of India, by order of the Chief Justice, dismissed the Government of West Bengal's 30 year litigation to get Brahmos classified as Hindus. The matter had previously been heard by an 11 Judge Constitution Bench of the Court (the second largest bench in the Court's history). As of 2007 the statutory minimum age for Brahmos to marry is 25(M)/21(F) versus 21(M)/18(or 15F) for Hindus.

It also supported social reform movements of people not directly attached to the *Samaj*, such as Pandit Iswar Chandra Vidyasagar's movement which promoted widow re-marriage.

Doctrine

The following doctrines, as noted in Renaissance of Hinduism, are common to all varieties and offshoots of the *Brahmo Samaj*:

Brahmo Samajists have no faith in any scripture as an authority.

Brahmo Samajists have no faith in Avatars.

Brahmo Samajists denounce polytheism and idol-worship.

Brahmo Samajists are against caste restrictions.

Brahmo Samajists make faith in the doctrines of Karma and Rebirth optional.

Principles of Brahmo Samaj

The following prime principles are accepted by the vast majority of Brahmos today.

On God: There is always Infinite Singularity - immanent and transcendant Singular Author and Preserver of Existence - He who is manifest everywhere and in everything, in the fire and in the water, in the smallest plant to the mightiest oak.

On Being: Being is created from Singularity. Being is renewed to Singularity. Being exists to be one (again) with Loving Singularity.

On Intelligent Existence: Righteous actions alone rule Existence against Chaos. Knowledge of pure Conscience (light within) is the One (Supreme) ruler of Existence with no symbol or intermediary.

On Love: Respect all creations and beings but never venerate (worship) them for only Singularity can be adored.

The 18th century was, perhaps, the darkest age in Indian history. An old, decadent polity was crumbling, engulfing the entire society in darkness, and no light of hope was visible anywhere. The Muslim rule was disintegrating, and that of the East India Company had not yet established itself. The result was an unprecedented political chaos and confusion.

The political disrder was not the only catastrophe that had befallen India. Of immeasurably greater consequence was the tragic fact that at this fateful hour, India had lost her links with her own supreme realizations, her universal and eternal thoughts. Indeed, all the vital links of the society lay paralysed. Urban and rural life, religious and educational institutions, law and administration, agriculture and industry, trade and commerce - all these were in a state of complete prostration. Dead, meaningless habits and decadent traditions stifled all creative efforts in the fields of art and culture, religion and politics. The stream of ancient Hindu ideals, based on the original scriptures - the Vedas and the Upanishads - had lost its way in the arid desert of superstition, bigotry and perversions. In place of critical analysis, there flourished unreasoned acceptance; instead of deference to authority after judgement, there ruled blind acceptance; where the torch of adventure had lighted the spirit, there reigned formal dogmatism. The Indian mind had become both lethargic and fearful. India had lost her youth.

At this crossroad of history, what India needed most was the advent of a man who would with one mighty sweep clear away the accumulated debris of othodoxy and unreason, who would rediscover India's imperishable thoughts and who, by doing so, would rekindle the spirit of the whole nation. This historical need was served by the emergence of the man who can truly be called the father of modern India - Rammohun Roy.

It was Renan who called Petrarch "the first modern mark", and by "modern man" he meant the freed individual who had achieved full emancipation of his spirit. Swami Vivekananda, another maker of modern India, attributed to Rammohun the same quality when he described him as "the first man of new, regenerate India".

The foundation of modern India that Rammohun laid was agreat synthesis - a synthesis among the three conflicting cultures, three conflicting civilizations - the Hindu, the Muslim and the Christian. Rammohun was the first to evolve a concord and convergence among the three, thus ushering in modern age which is characterised by the evolution of a composite nationality and a synthetic civilization in India. Indeed, he went further, On the same lines of convergence, and through the experiences of his universal personality, he saw in the clarity of this synthetic vision, the solution of the larger problem of international culture and civilization. Rammohun understood as nobody had else had done before him, that human progress lies not in separation among nations but in the fraternity of interdependance of individuals and nations evolved through rational synthesis of cultures and civilizations. To this synthetic vision of Rammohun in the spheres of religion and culture, the Indian Renaissance of the 19th century owes its origin and birth. Indeed, there was not a single aspect of India's life - political, social, economic, religious and cultural - which was not shaken out of stupor, and rendered dynamic by the touch of this mighty personality.

Historically, the Renaissance signifies a many-sided, complex movement, a critical and creative outburst of human spirit to free itself from the worn-out moral and religious ideas of the time. It is a movement in which the intellect finds its freedom, the imagination spreads its wings, the narrow, restricted existence makes a strenuous effort to break down the barriers of the old society, and seeks new sources of intellectual and imaginative enjoyment - both in the ancient and in the contemporary experience of man.

In the opening years of the 19th century, ideas acquired a role in the life of Calcutta which is still there. Before that, the preoccupation was making money, and that too quickly, for fear of Portugese piracy on the Hooghly estuary, or of Dutch and French attacks by sea, or of Maratha and Moghul inroads by land. All the important residents had come from elsewhere: the English acreoss the seas, the Armenians overland, and Indians from villages and towns both near and distant. Though the Setts and Basaks had been in Sutanati and Govindapur long enough to identify themselves with the growing city, Calcutta was important but lacked an identity ...

Among the problems that Rammohun Roy faced, the priority belonged to social reform rather than man's position in nature. To him and several thinkers after him, religion, social reforms and politics were so intermixed that philosophy received little attention. The most important issue for Rammohun was that of identity. Society in Calcutta, as well as throughout the country, was ascriptive. Birth determined one's religion as well as one's ritual status; no individual; or group could change caste or ritual status. And change of religion invited censure. Caste identity was indeed difficult to obliterate. However, before his departure for England, Rammohun made sure that the trust deed of the first Brahmo temple - executed on January 23, 1830 - defined it as "a place of public meeting of all people without distinction" ...

Ishwarchandra Vidyasagar was the most outspokenly forthright of all in the rejection of Indian schools of thought, highlighted by his 1835 letter to the Board of Education on the subject of teachings at Sanskrit College. He maintained that truth had two heads - one according to the 'Empiricists' (such as Locke and Hume), and the other in consonance with Vedanta, Sankhya and Nyaya. In the same letter, he rejected the proposal to teach his pupils Berkeley's Idealism. Vidyasagar was different from most Indian thinkers. After the 1867 famine, he disputed the contention that God was compassionate; for He could not otherwise let so many men, women and children die because of the failure of the monsoon, no fault of theirs. Normally, Vidyasagar did not bother himself with divinity, and the provocation for this utterance has not been traced.

Rarely did he quote the scriptures and the shashtras, except when he chanced upon one in support of the reforms he advocated.

For 40 years (1840 to 1880), Debendranath Tagore led that section of the elite which immersed themselves with beliefs and ideas. He had reacted sharply to the prevalent Christian proselytisation, and revived the Brahmo movement which had lost its vigour after Rammohun's death. He allowed caste distinctions to continue, even though he may not have approved of them personally. Debendranath was a Vedantist who put his trust in the Upanishad which Rammohun had recommended to Brahmos as satisfying modern consciousness.

Akshaykumar Datta, a young member of the Brahmo Samaj, impressed Debendranath Tagore with his sharp intellect. In 1850, Datta perdsuaded Debendranath and the Samaj to accept the proposition that the Vedas were not infallible. Yet Debendranath's continued to believe in Divine Inspiration. Ten years later, he conferred the honorific "Brahmabandhab" on another young man - Keshubchandra Sen (1837-1884), who joined the Brahmo Samaj in 1857 after it had ceased to subscribe to the infallibility of the Vedas. Little was expected from his talks with Dayanand Saraswati - the founder of the Arya Samaj - who upheld the infallibility of the Upanishads, the caste hierarchy and cow worship. The schism in the Brahmo Samaj that Keshubchandra Sen led in 1865 disowned caste difference, but the word 'Arya' or 'Aryan' was emotively venerated ...

We do not know whether Akshaykumar Datta and Keshubchandra Sen were friends, but we do know that Vidyasagar was friendly towards Datta. It was a tolewrant age, for the ostracism faced by Rammohun and the Derozians had ended, and the persecution of the Brahmos had not yet begun. Ramkrishna looked with respect towards Debendranath Tagore, Vidyasagar and Keshubchandra Sen, and paid them vists. From 1870, religious and political personalities pushed philosophy to the rear. August Comte's Positivism had found adherents in men like Dwarkanath Mitter and Jogen Ghosh, who conversed in drawing rooms, while religious leaders like Keshubchandra Sen and Vivekananda or political leaders like Surendranath Banerjee and Aurobindo waxed eloquent before impressive gatherings ...

The 1872 Civil Marriages Act made it obligatory for Brahmos - parties to inter-caste marriages and remarrying of widows - to declare themselves as non-Hindu. Meanwhile, the incidence of abhorrent practices associatd with Hinduism were declining. The burning of widows and infanticide were now penal offences. Child marriage was no longer rife amongst the educated. The need for a Hindu to be apologetic about his religion was lessening. After Vivekanada's exposition of Hinduism at the World Congress of Religion at Chicago in 1893, there was a resurgence of confidence amongst Hindus ...

The Industrial Revolution touched Calcutta around the 1850s and accelarated the influx of people from other towns and villages. The city had been receiving people since 1710, but at a rate which permitted the absorption in line with the prevailing customs. Accelaration made the immigrant a factor in the city's life. The immigrant shed caste habits and prejudices, but in turn moderated the townspeoples' departures from orthodoxy.

At the same time, modernisation tended to reduce the hold that religion exerted on the citizen. Scientific investigations and political activities had begun. In a sense, scientific explorations had begun in 1784 with the founding of the Asiatic Society of Bengal, followed by the laying of the Botanical Garden in 1787, the institution of the Botanical Survey in 1797, the Geological Survey in 1846, and the establishment of the Museum in 1814. These institutions served the European residents only. A few Indians, mostly Sanskrit scholars, were associated with the researches of the Asiatic Society. They helped Europe's discovery of India and Europe's Oriental Renaissance. The feedback from these developments started reaching Calcutta fro 1860 onwards, and strengthened religious revivalism and nationalism.

One aspect of this feedback from Europe was the interest by German Idealists (Kant and his succesors) in India's 'speculative' philosophy. That fueled a revived interest in the Upanishads and Vedas. And Vivekananda's enthusiastic listeners abroad led to further acclaim at home.

Interest in 'Positivism' may be ascribed to three unrelated motivations. One, it was more recent than 'Empiricism', and could be attractive on that account to those aspiring for distinction in a colonial city. Two, nascent nationalists would turn to any source other than the English for inspiration. Positivism had originated in France, and it is known that one if its pioneers in Calcutta took pride in having read the original French texts. Lastly, but probably of greatest significance, was the fast that one of its British propagators declared that it was "capable of giving a reason for respecting Hindi social institutions", including the caste system.

Brahmos and Derozians, influenced by 'Empiricism', were critical of Hindu social systems, especially the caste system. Positivism set out to be respectful to the caste system, and this was its attraction for some Calcuttans. The best known among them are Bhudeb Mukherjee and Bankimchandra Chatterjee. Neither of them joined the Positivist Society, though they had friends in it...

Bhudeb Mukherjee was an essayist and repected for his eruditeness, although not as widely read as Bankimchandra Chatterjee. The 1880s was a decade of resurgent Hinduism as much as the fifties focussed on rationalism and the sixties of advancing Brahmoism. Vidyasagar and Akshaykumar Datta provided the setting for Michael Madhusudan Dutt'a cosmopolitanism in the fifties. In the sixties, Keshubchandra Sen told enthusiastic and appreciative audiences that India's spirituality and Europe's science matched each other as the vital complementary components of the modern world.

The seventies had seen the preliminaris of a Hindu revival in the Hindu Melas, but the requisite intellectual vigour was available only in the eighties, which provided nationalism with the energy it had so far lacked. Bhudeb Mukherjee and Bankimchandra Chatterjee found their efforts supplemented by those of Vivekananda, till their achievements were dwarfed by the younger man's...

Bhudeb Mukherjee was an advocate of Hindi, which the Arya Samaj in 1875 had adopted as the language of propagation. Hindi became the language of the lower courts in the Central Province (now Madhya Pradesh) in 1882 and in Bihar in 1883. Mukherjee, then posted in Bihar, had a role in the administration's acceptance of Hindi. Chatterjee was also posted in Bihar at this time. Hindi became the national language in 1947.

In the novel 'Anandamath', Bankimchandra Chatterjee provided later generations of activist nationalists with a model for change. The song Bande Mataram occupies the position of the second national anthem now, but was the sole one between 1905 and 1947. It was a cry of defiance and a slogan of revolt during the freedom struggle.

Vivekananda turned to religion, provoked by Vidyasagar's observation after the 1867 famine, that God could not be mercifuland compassionate. Whatever the antecedents of the observation, it launched vidyasagar on the social service that Hinduism had not known before. Hinduism lacked organization for succour to the sick, bereaved, destitute or struck by natural calmity, or to impart education to the young. Little can be done by an individual in a situation created by a famine, but there is considerable scope for charity or social service in everyday life. Charity was quite absent in Hindu life. The unfortunate and the poor were despised as paying for their sins in a previous birth - a corollary to the belief in the transmigration of soul.

Opinions differ whether or not Vivekananda found evidence of a compassionate God, but he did furnish Hinduism with an organization similar to what the Christians had. It was and is named the 'Ramakrishna Mission', named and organized on the model of its Christian counterparts.

It had a predecessor. In 1843 three Derozians - Kisorichand Mitra, Ramgopal Ghosh and Pearychand Mitra - combined with the atheist Akshaykumar Datta to form the Hindu Philanthropic Society. In spite of the support of a rich man like Ramgopal Ghosh, the Society foundered. Traditionally, charity was meant exclusivelu for the Brahmins ...

More schools of thought competed for adherents in the city in the second half of the 19th century than the first. From 1850 the conservative leadership devolved on Debendranath Tagore. Technically, he was a Brahno, but of that section which would not break with Hindu caste rules.

However, not all the softening of attitudes was on the Brahmo side. Ramakrishna Paramahansa (1836-1886), the outstanding Hindu pietist who had come to Calcutta in 1855, humble as he was, called on Debendranath Tagore and Keshubchandra Sen, even on Vidyasagar. The visit to Vidyasagar ended with civilities and nothing else, though Vidyasagar, when told by Ramakrishna that he had come to the "sea" (sagar), replied: "Since you have come to the sea, take some salt water back with you." Ramakrishna did not stop at visits. He took up an idea underlying all Brahmo thinking from Rammohun to Keshubchandra Sen, that of the underlying unity of all religions which could lead to the combining of the good points of all. Ramakrishna experimented with living in succession as a follower of each of the major religions. He concluded that he was most comfortable being a Hindu, as he was home with its mores; the inference was not that Hinduism was superior to all other religions, but that there was no need to switch over from one faith to another; to emphasize to all those restive with Hinduism to stay in the religion they were born in. His disciple, Vivekananda (1836-1902), continued Ramakrishna's efforts, and after Chicago in 1893, was able to secure for Hinduism a recognition which staved off attacks by Christian Evangelists and dissatisfied Hindus...

Michael Madhusudan Datta (1824-1891) became a Christian in 1843 to escape the confines of the Hindu society, ate beef and drank wine publicly and demonstrably, and turned Meghnad, brother of the arch-fiend Ravana in Ramayana, into a hero. He did not take up the role of a reformer, or even a thinker. Instead he devoted his labours to poetry. Vidyasagar, the intellectual leader, saw Madhusudhan Dutt as a pioneer of modern Bengali and encouraged him. Vidyasagar bcame the prinicipal benefactor of Dutt, in spite of being addressed by Dutt with the words "though you are a Hindu ..."; Vidyasagar took no offence.

Madhusudan Dutt's main contribution as a poet and playwright was to broaden the outlook and sympathies of the Bengali reader and to induce him to to see that interpretations other than the conventional were possible. Bengali was just achieving recognition as a literary language; the date usually assigned is 1855. Dutt introduced into it an awareness of Greek and Latin classics. He also made a plea for greater use of Muslim topics. Dutt was cosmopolitan in more varied aspects of life than the religious. Bengali cosmopolitanism was to flower about 30 years after Dutt's death, but its seeds were sown by him through his literary work after 1855. The artist and writer - as a propagator of ideas - came to substitute for the religious and social reformer.

Ram Mohun also spelled RAMMOHUN, RAMMOHAN, OR RAM MOHAN Indian religious, social, and educational reformer who challenged traditional Hindu culture and indicated the lines of progress for Indian society under British rule. He is sometimes called the father of modern India.

He was born in British-ruled Bengal to a prosperous family of the Brahman caste. Little is known of his early life and education, but he seems to have developed unorthodox religious ideas at an early age. As a youth he traveled widely outside Bengal and mastered several languages—Sanskrit, Persian, Arabic, and later Hebrew, Greek, and English, in addition to his native Bengali and Hindi.

Roy supported himself by moneylending, managing his small estates, and speculating in British East India Company bonds. In 1805 he was employed by John Digby, a lower company official. Through Digby he was introduced to Western culture and literature. For the next 10 years Roy drifted in and out of British East India Company service as Digby's assistant.

Roy continued his religious studies throughout this period. In 1803 he composed a tract denouncing India's religious divisions and superstition. As a remedy for these ills, he advocated a monotheistic Hinduism in which reason guides the adherent to "... the Absolute Originator who is the first principle of all religions." He sought a philosophical basis for his religious beliefs in the Upanishads and Vedas, translating these ancient Sanskrit treatises into Bengali, Hindi, and English and writing summaries and treatises on them. The central theme of these texts, for Roy, was the worship of the Supreme God, beyond human knowledge, who supports the universe. By translating the sacred Sanskrit Upanishads into modern Bengali, Roy violated a long-standing tradition, but, in appreciation of his translations, the French Société Asiatique in 1824 elected him to an honorary membership.

In 1815 Roy founded the short-lived Atmiya-Sabha (Friendly Society) to propagate his doctrines of monotheistic Hinduism. He became interested in Christianity and learned Hebrew and Greek in order to read the Old and New Testaments. In 1820 he published the ethical teachings of Christ, excerpted from the four Gospels, under the title Precepts of Jesus, the Guide to Peace and Happiness.

9

BANGLADESH

Bangladesh, officially the People's Republic of Bangladesh [*Gônoprojatontri Bangladesh*) is a country in South Asia. It is bordered by India on all sides except for a small border with Burma (Myanmar) to the far southeast and by the Bay of Bengal to the south. Together with the Indian state of West Bengal, it makes up the ethno-linguistic region of Bengal. The name *Bangladesh* means "Country of Bengal" in the official Bengali language.

The borders of present-day Bangladesh were established with the partition of Bengal and India in 1947, when the region became the eastern wing of the newly formed Pakistan. However, it was separated from the western wing by 1,600 km (994 mi) of Indian territory. Political and linguistic discrimination as well as economic neglect led to popular agitations against West Pakistan, which led to the war for independence in 1971 and the establishment of Bangladesh. After independence, the new state endured famines, natural disasters and widespread poverty, as well as political turmoil and military coups. The restoration of democracy in 1991 has been followed by relative calm and economic progress.

Bangladesh is the seventh most populous country and is among the most densely populated countries in the world with a high poverty rate. However, per-capita (inflation-adjusted) GDP has more than doubled since 1975, and the poverty rate has fallen by 20% since the early 1990s. The country is listed among the "Next Eleven" economies. Dhaka, the capital, and other urban centers have been the driving force behind this growth.

Geographically, the country straddles the fertile Ganges-Brahmaputra Delta and is subject to annual monsoon floods and cyclones. It has the longest unbroken sea beach in the world in the Cox's Bazaar. Bangladesh is a parliamentary democracy with an elected parliament called the Jatiyo Sangshad. The country is a member of the Commonwealth of Nations, the OIC, SAARC, BIMSTEC, and the D-8. As the World Bank notes in its July 2005 Country Brief, the country has made significant progress in human development in the areas of literacy, gender parity in schooling and reduction of population growth. However, Bangladesh continues to face a number of major challenges, including widespread political and bureaucratic corruption, economic competition relative to the world, serious overpopulation, widespread poverty, and an increasing danger of hydrologic shocks brought on by ecological vulnerability to climate change.

Remnants of civilization in the greater Bengal region date back four thousand years, when the region was settled by Dravidian, Tibeto-Burman, and Austro-Asiatic peoples. The exact origin of the word "Bangla" or "Bengal" is unknown, though it is believed to be derived from *Bang*, the Dravidian-speaking tribe that settled in the area around the year 1000 BC.

The kingdom of Gangaridai was formed from at least the 7th century BC, which later united with Bihar under the Magadha, Nanda, Mauryan and Sunga Empires. Bengal was later part of the Gupta Empire and Harsha Empire from the 3rd to the 6th centuries CE. Following its collapse, a dynamic Bengali named Shashanka founded an impressive short-lived kingdom. Shashanka is considered the first independent king in the history of Bangladesh.

After a period of anarchy, the Buddhist Pala dynasty ruled the region for four hundred years, followed by a shorter reign of the Hindu Sena dynasty. Islam was introduced to Bengal in the 12th century by Arab Muslim merchants; Sufi missionaries and subsequent Muslim conquests helped spread Islam throughout the region.

Bakhtiar Khilji, a Turkic general, defeated Lakshman Sen of the Sena dynasty and conquered large parts of Bengal in the year 1204. The region was ruled by dynasties of Sultans and land lords Bhuiyan for the next few hundred years. By the 16th century the Mughal Empire controlled Bengal and Dhaka became an important provincial centre of Mughal administration.

European traders arrived late in the 15th century, and their influence grew until the British East India Company gained control of Bengal following the Battle of Plassey in 1757. The bloody rebellion of 1857 – known as the Sepoy Mutiny – resulted in transfer of authority to the crown with a British viceroy running the administration. During colonial rule, famine racked the Indian subcontinent many times, including the Great Bengal famine of 1943 that claimed 3 million lives.

Between 1905 and 1911, an abortive attempt was made to divide the province of Bengal into two zones, with Dhaka being the capital of the eastern zone. When India was partitioned in 1947, Bengal was partitioned along religious lines (for the majority Muslims), with the western part going to India and the eastern part joining Pakistan as a province called East Bengal (later renamed East Pakistan), with its capital at Dhaka.

In 1950, land reform was accomplished in East Bengal with the abolishment of the feudal zamindari system. However, despite the economic and demographic weight of the east, Pakistan's government and military were largely dominated by the upper classes from the west. The Bengali Language Movement of 1952 was the first sign of friction between the two wings of Pakistan.

Dissatisfaction with the central government over economic and cultural issues continued to rise through the next decade, during which the Awami League emerged as the political voice of the Bengali-speaking population. It agitated for autonomy in the 1960s, and in 1966, its president Sheikh Mujibur Rahman was jailed; he was released in 1969, after an unprecedented popular uprising.

In 1970, a massive cyclone devastated the coast of East Pakistan, killing up to half a million people, and the central government responded poorly. The Bengali population's anger was compounded when Sheikh Mujibur Rahman, whose Awami League won a majority in Parliament in the 1970 elections, was blocked from taking office.

After staging compromise talks with Mujib, President Yahya Khan arrested him on the early hours of March 26, 1971, and launched Operation Searchlight, a sustained military assault on East Pakistan. Yahya's methods were extremely bloody, and the violence of the war resulted in many civilian deaths . Chief targets included intellectuals and Hindus, and about ten million refugees fled to neighbouring India. Estimates of those massacred throughout the war range from three hundred thousand to 3 million.

Before his arrest by the Pakistan Army, Sk. Mujibur Rahman formally declared the independence of Bangladesh and directed everyone to fight till the last soldier of the Pakistan army was evicted from East Pakistan. Awami League leaders set up a government-in-exile in Calcutta, India. The exile government formally took oath at Mujib Nagar in Kustia district of East Pakistan on April 17, 1971 with Tajuddin Ahmad as the first Prime Minister.

The Bangladesh Liberation War lasted for nine months. The Bangladesh Forces formed within 11 sectors led by General M.A.G. Osmani consisting of Bengali Regulars and Mukti Bahini conducted a massive guerilla war against the Pakistan Forces with all out support from the Indian Armed Forces. Jointly the Mitro Bahini achieved a decisive victory over Pakistan on December 16, 1971, with Indian Armed Forces taking over 90,000 prisoners of war.

After its independence, Bangladesh became a parliamentary democracy, with Mujib as the Prime Minister. In the 1973 parliamentary elections, the Awami League gained an absolute majority. A nationwide famine occurred during 1973 and 1974, and in early 1975, Mujib initiated a one-party socialist rule with his newly formed BAKSAL. On August 15, 1975, Mujib with most of his family members were assassinated by mid-level military officers.

A series of bloody coups and counter-coups in the following three months culminated in the ascent to power of General Ziaur Rahman, who reinstated multi-party politics & founded the Bangladesh Nationalist Party (BNP). Zia's rule ended when he was assassinated in 1981 by elements of the military. Bangladesh's next major ruler was General Hossain Mohammad Ershad, who gained power in a bloodless coup in 1982 and ruled until 1990, when he was forced to resign after a massive revolt of all major political parties and the public, joined with pressure from western donors (which was a major shift in international policy after the end of communism).

Since then, Bangladesh has reverted to a parliamentary democracy. Zia's widow, Khaleda Zia, led the Bangladesh Nationalist Party to parliamentary victory at the general election in 1991 and became the first female Prime Minister in Bangladesh's history. However, the Awami League, headed by Sheikh Hasina, one of Mujib's surviving daughters, clinched power at the next election in 1996 but lost to the Bangladesh Nationalist Party again in 2001.

On January 11, 2007, following widespread political unrest, a caretaker government was appointed to administer the next general election. The country had suffered from extensive corruption, disorder and political violence. The new caretaker government has made it a priority to root out corruption from all levels of government. To this end, many notable politicians and officials, along with large numbers of lesser officials and party members, have been arrested on corruption charges. The caretaker government held a fair and free election on December 29, 2008. Awami League's Sheikh Hasina won the elections with a landslide victory and took the oath of Prime Minister on January 6, 2009.

Bangladesh is a unitary state and parliamentary democracy. Direct elections in which all citizens, aged 18 or over, can vote are held every five years for the unicameral parliament known as Jatiya Sangsad. The parliamentary building is known as the *Jatiyo Sangshad Bhaban* and was designed by architect Louis Kahn. Currently the parliament has 345 members including 45 reserved seats for women, elected from single-member constituencies. The Prime Minister, as the head of government, forms the cabinet and runs the day-to-day affairs of state. While the Prime Minister is formally appointed by the President, he or she must be an MP who commands the confidence of the majority of parliament. The President is the head of state but mainly a ceremonial post elected by the parliament.

However the President's powers are substantially expanded during the tenure of a caretaker government, which is responsible for the conduct of elections and transfer of power. The officers of the caretaker government must be non-partisan and are given three months to complete their task. This transitional arrangement is an innovation that was pioneered by Bangladesh in its 1991 election and then institutionalized in 1996 through its 13th constitutional amendment.

The Constitution of Bangladesh was drafted in 1972 and has undergone fourteen amendments. The highest judicial body is the Supreme Court. Justices are appointed by the President. The judicial and law enforcement institutions are weak. Separation of powers, judicial from executive was finally implemented on the 1st of November, 2007. It is expected that this separation will make the judiciary stronger and impartial. Laws are loosely based on English common law, but family laws such as marriage and inheritance are based on religious scripts, and therefore differ between religious communities.

The two major parties in Bangladesh are the Bangladesh Awami League and the Bangladesh Nationalist Party (BNP). BNP is led by Khaleda Zia and finds its allies among Islamist parties like Jamaat-e-Islami Bangladesh and Islami Oikya Jot, while Sheikh Hasina's Awami League aligns with leftist and secularist parties. Hasina and Zia are bitter rivals who have dominated politics for over 15 years; each is related to one of the leaders of the independence movement. Another important player is the Jatiya Party, headed by former military dictator Ershad. The Awami League-BNP rivalry has been bitter and punctuated by protests, violence and murder. Student politics is particularly strong in Bangladesh, a legacy from the liberation movement era. Almost all parties have highly active student wings, and student leaders have been elected to the Parliament.

Two radical terrorist organizations, Jagrata Muslim Janata Bangladesh (JMJB) and Jama'atul Mujahideen Bangladesh (JMB), were banned in February 2005. Several small-scale bomb attacks taking place since 1999 have been blamed on those groups, and dozens of suspected members have been detained in security operations, including the heads of those two parties in 2006. The masterminds were tried and executed. The Bangladesh government won praise from world leaders, including Western leaders, for its strong anti-terrorist stance.

The January 22, 2007 election was postponed indefinitely and emergency law declared in January 11, 2007 as Army backed caretaker government of Fakhruddin Ahmed aimed to prepare a new voter list and crack down on corruption. They also assisted the interim Government of Bangladesh in a drive against corruption, which resulted in Bangladesh's position in the Transparency International's Corruption Index changed from the very bottom, where they had been for 3 year in a row, to 147th in just 1 year.

A large alliance led by the Bangladesh Awami League won the December 29, 2008 poll, in a landslide victory. They got 230 seats among 300 seats in the parliament. On 31 July 2009 Prime Minister Sheikh Hasina expanded the Bangladeshi cabinet to bring the total size to 44.

Bangladesh pursues a moderate foreign policy that places heavy reliance on multinational diplomacy, especially at the United Nations. In 1974 Bangladesh joined both the Commonwealth of Nations and the United Nations and has since been elected to serve two terms on the Security Council in 1978–1979 and 2000–2001. In the 1980s, Bangladesh played a lead role in founding the South Asian Association for Regional Cooperation (SAARC) in order to expand relations with other South Asian states. Since the founding of SAARC 1985, a Bangladeshi has held the post of Secretary General on two occasions.

Bangladesh's most important and complex foreign relationships are with India. These relationships are informed by historical and cultural ties and form an important part of the domestic political discourse.

Bangladesh's relationship with India began on a positive note because of India's assistance in the independence war and reconstruction. Throughout the years, relations between both countries have fluctuated for a number of reasons. A major source of tension between Bangladesh and India is the Farakka Dam. In 1975, India constructed a dam on the Ganges River 11 miles (18 km) from the Bangladeshi border. Bangladesh alleges that the dam diverts much needed water from Bangladesh and adds a man-made disaster to the country already plagued by natural disasters. The dam also has terrible ecological consequences. On the other hand, India has voiced concerns about anti-Indian separatists and Islamic militants allegedly being harboured across their 2,500-mile (4,000 km) border, as well as the flow of illegal migrants, and is building a fence along most of it. But at the 2007 SAARC meeting both nations pledged to work cooperatively on security, economic and border issues .

The current strength of the army is around 200,000 including reservists, the air force 22,000, and navy 14,950. In addition to traditional defense roles, the military has been called on to provide support to civil authorities for disaster relief and internal security during periods of political unrest. Bangladesh is not currently active in any ongoing war, but it did contribute 2,300 troops to the coalition that fought in Operation Desert Storm in 1991 and Bangladesh is consistently a top contributor to UN peacekeeping forces around the world. As of May 2007,

Bangladesh had major deployments in Democratic Republic of Congo, Liberia, Sudan, Timor-Leste and Côte d'Ivoire. Presently Bangladesh is the 2nd largest troop contributor country to the UN.

Bangladesh enjoys relatively warm ties with the People's Republic of China which has, particularly in the past decade, increased economic cooperation with the South Asian nation. Between 2006 and 2007, trade between the two nations rose by 28.5% and there have been agreements to grant various Bangladeshi commodities tariff-free access to the Chinese market. Cooperation between the Military of Bangladesh and the People's Liberation Army is also increasing, with joint military agreements signed and Bangladesh procuring Chinese arms which range from small arms to large naval surface combatants such as the Chinese Type 053H1 Missile Frigate.

Divisions are subdivided into districts (*zila*). There are 64 districts in Bangladesh, each further subdivided into *upazila* (subdistricts) or *thana*. The area within each police station, except for those in metropolitan areas, is divided into several *unions*, with each union consisting of multiple villages. In the metropolitan areas, police stations are divided into wards, which are further divided into *mahallas*. There are no elected officials at the divisional, district or upazila levels, and the administration is composed only of government officials. Direct elections are held for each union (or ward), electing a chairperson and a number of members. In 1997, a parliamentary act was passed to reserve three seats (out of twelve) in every union for female candidates.

Dhaka is the capital and largest city of Bangladesh. Other major cities include Chittagong, Khulna, Rajshahi, Sylhet, Barisal, Bogra, Comilla, Mymensingh and Rangpur. These cities have mayoral elections, while other municipalities elect a chairperson. Mayors and chairpersons are elected for a span of five years.

Bangladesh is in the low-lying Ganges–Brahmaputra River Delta or Ganges Delta. This delta is formed by the confluence of the Ganges (local name Padma or *Pôdda*), Brahmaputra (Jamuna or *Jomuna*), and Meghna rivers and their respective tributaries. The Ganges unites with the Jamuna (main channel of the Brahmaputra) and later joins the Meghna to eventually empty into the Bay of Bengal. The alluvial soil deposited by these rivers has created some of the most fertile plains in the world. Bangladesh has 58 trans-boundary rivers, making water issues politically complicated to resolve – in most cases as the lower riparian state to India. Most parts of Bangladesh are less than 12 m (39.4 ft) above the sea level, and it is believed that about 50% of the land would be flooded if the sea level were to rise by 1 m (3.28 ft).

In south east Bangladesh experiments have been done since the sixties to 'build with nature'. By implementing cross dams, the natural accretion of silt has created new land. With Dutch funding, the Bangladeshi government began to help develop this new land in the late 1970s. The effort has since become a multiagency operation building roads, culverts, embankments, cyclone shelters, toilets and ponds, as well as distributing land to settlers. By fall 2010, the program will have allotted some 27,000 acres (10,927 ha) to 21,000 families.

Straddling the Tropic of Cancer, Bangladeshi climate is tropical with a mild winter from October to March, a hot, humid summer from March to June. A warm and humid monsoon season lasts from June to October and supplies most of the country's rainfall. Natural calamities, such as floods, tropical cyclones, tornadoes, and tidal bores occur almost every year,[49] combined with the effects of deforestation, soil degradation and erosion. Cox's Bazar, south of the city of Chittagong, has a beach that stretches uninterrupted over 120 kilometres (75 mi).

In September 1998, Bangladesh saw the most severe flooding in modern world history. As the Brahmaputra, Ganges and Meghna spilt over and swallowed 300,000 houses, 9,700 kilometres (6,027 mi) of road and 2,700 kilometres (1,678 mi) of embankment 1,000 people were killed and 30 million more were made homeless with 135,000 cattle killed, 50 square kilometres

(19.3 sq mi) of land destroyed and 11,000 kilometres (6,835 mi) of roads damaged or destroyed. Two-thirds of the country was underwater. There were several reasons for the severity of the flooding. Firstly, there were unusually high monsoon rains. Secondly, the Himalayas shed off an equally unusually high amount of melt water that year. Thirdly, trees that usually would have intercept rain water had been cut down for firewood or to make space for animals.

Bangladesh is now widely recognized to be one of the countries most vulnerable to climate change. Natural hazards that come from increased rainfall, rising sea levels, and tropical cyclones are expected to increase as climate change, each seriously affecting agriculture, water & food security, human health and shelter. It is believed that in the coming decades the rising sea level alone will create more than 20 million climate refugees.

Bangladeshi water is contaminated with arsenic frequently because of the high arsenic contents in the soil. Up to 77 million people are exposed to toxic arsenic from drinking water.

A major part of the coastline comprises a marshy jungle, the Sundarbans, the largest mangrove forest in the world and home to diverse flora and fauna, including the Royal Bengal Tiger. In 1997, this region was declared endangered. The Magpie Robin is the National Bird of Bangladesh and it is common and known as the *Doyel* or *Doel* . It is a widely used symbol in Bangladesh, appearing on currency notes and a landmark in the city of Dhaka is named as the *Doyel Chatwar* (meaning: Doyel Square).The national flower of the country is water lily, which is known as *Shapla*. The national fruit is jackfruit, which in Bengali is known as *Kathal*.

Despite continuous domestic and international efforts to improve economic and demographic prospects, Bangladesh remains a developing nation. Its per capita income in 2008 was US$520 compared to the world average of $10,200.

Jute was once the economic engine of the country. Its share of the world export market peaked in the Second World War and the late 1940s at 80% and even in the early 1970s accounted for 70% of its export earnings. However, polypropylene products began to substitute for jute products worldwide and the jute industry started to decline. Bangladesh grows very significant quantities of rice, tea and mustard.

Although two-thirds of Bangladeshis are farmers, more than three quarters of Bangladesh's export earnings come from the garment industry, which began attracting foreign investors in the 1980s due to cheap labour and low conversion cost. In 2002, the industry exported US$5 billion worth of products. The industry now employs more than 3 million workers, 90% of whom are women. A large part of foreign currency earnings also comes from the remittances sent by expatriates living in other countries.

Obstacles to growth include frequent cyclones and floods, inefficient state-owned enterprises, mismanaged port facilities, a growth in the labour force that has outpaced jobs, inefficient use of energy resources (such as natural gas), insufficient power supplies, slow implementation of economic reforms, political infighting and corruption. According to the World Bank, "among Bangladesh's most significant obstacles to growth are poor governance and weak public institutions."

Despite these hurdles, the country has achieved an average annual growth rate of 5% since 1990, according to the World Bank. Bangladesh has seen expansion of its middle class, and its consumer industry has also grown. In December 2005, four years after its report on the emerging "BRIC" economies (Brazil, Russia, India, and China), Goldman Sachs named Bangladesh one of the "Next Eleven", along with Egypt, Indonesia, Vietnam and seven other countries. Bangladesh has seen a dramatic increase in foreign direct investment.

Youth employment also poses a problem, adding to the frustration that often leads to violence among students and young people. However, improvements are being made. NGOs such as BRAC work towards the inclusion of young men and especially young women in the workforce. BRAC's Adolescent Development Program, for example, provided lifeskills and livelihood trainings. Almost 80 % of the participants were female. Moving ahead in Bangladesh

A number of multinational corporations and local big business houses such as Beximco, Square, Akij Group, Ispahani, Navana Group, Transcom Group, Habib Group, KDS Group, Dragon Group and multinationals such as Unocal Corporation and Chevron, have made major investments, with the natural gas sector being a priority. In December 2005, the Central Bank of Bangladesh projected GDP growth around 6.5%.

One significant contributor to the development of the economy has been the widespread propagation of microcredit by Muhammad Yunus (awarded the Nobel peace prize in 2006) through the Grameen Bank. By the late 1990s, Grameen Bank had 2.3 million members, along with 2.5 million members of other similar organisations.

Recent (2005–2007) estimates of Bangladesh's population range from 142 to 159 million, making it the 7th most populous nation in the world. With a land area of 144,000 square kilometres (56,000 sq mi), ranked 94th, the population density is remarkable. A striking comparison is offered by the fact that Russia's population is slightly smaller even though Russia has a land area of 17.5 million square kilometers, at least 120 times bigger than Bangladesh.

Bangladesh has the highest population density in the world, excluding a handful of city-states and small countries such as Malta. Bangladesh's population growth was among the highest in the world in the 1960s and 1970s, when the country grew from 50 to 90 million, but with the promotion of birth control in the 1980s, the growth rate slowed. The population is relatively young, with the 0–25 age group comprising 60%, while 3% are 65 or older. Life expectancy is 63 years for both males and females.

The majority ethnic group of Bangladesh are the Bengali people, comprising 98% of the population. The remainder are mostly Bihari migrants and indigenous tribal groups. There are thirteen tribal groups located in the Chittagong Hill Tracts, the most populous of the tribes are the Chakmas. The region has been a source of ethnic tension since the inception of Bangladesh.

The largest tribal groups outside the Hill Tracts are the Santhals and the Garos (Achiks). There are also Kaibartta, Meitei, Mundas, Oraons, and Zomi ethnic groups. Human trafficking has been a lingering problem in Bangladesh and illegal immigration has remained a cause of friction with Burma and India.

The official and most widely used language in Bangladesh, as in West Bengal, is Bengali or Bangla, an Indo-Aryan language of Sanskrit origin with its own script. English is used as second language among the middle and upper classes and in higher education. Since a President Order in 1987, Bengali is used for all official correspondence except those that are to foreign recipients.

Health and education levels have recently improved as poverty levels have decreased. Most Bangladeshis are rural, living on subsistence farming. Health problems abound, ranging from surface water contamination, to arsenic contamination of groundwater, and diseases including malaria, leptospirosis and dengue. The literacy rate in Bangladesh is approximately 41%. There is gender disparity, though, as literacy rates are 50% among men and 31% among women, according to a 2004 UNICEF estimate. Literacy has gone up due to many programmes introduced in the country. Among the most successful ones are the *Food for education* (FFE) programme introduced in 1993, and a stipend programme for women at the primary and secondary levels.

The major religion practiced in Bangladesh is Islam (89.7%) and a sizable minority adheres to Hinduism (9.2%). The majority of Muslims are Sunni, while the rest are either Shia, Ahmadiyya or Sufi. Ethnic Biharis are predominantly Shia

Muslims. Other religious groups include Buddhists (0.7%, mostly Theravada), Christians (0.3%, mostly of the Roman Catholic denomination), and Animists (0.1%).

Bangladesh ranks fourth after Indonesia, Pakistan, and India by the number of Muslims, with over 130 million. Islam is the state religion of Bangladesh, but other religions may also be practiced in harmony. The United Nations has recognised the country mainly as a moderate Muslim democratic country.

In 2010, the High Court has forbidden punishments from Islamic edicts or fatwas and ruled that any person who issues or executes them will be punished. This follows several filings by human rights organisations which came in response to often brutal punishments on women found guilty of committing adultery, having a child out of wedlock or for talking to people of another faith ."

Reflecting the long history of the region, Bangladesh has a culture that encompasses elements both old and new. The Bengali language boasts a rich literary heritage, which Bangladesh shares with the Indian state of West Bengal. The earliest literary text in Bengali is the 8th century Charyapada. Medieval Bengali literature was often either religious (e.g. Chandidas), or adapted from other languages (e.g. Alaol). Bengali literature reached its full expression in the nineteenth century, with its greatest icons being poets Rabindranath Tagore and Kazi Nazrul Islam. Bangladesh also has a long tradition in folk literature, for example *Maimansingha Gitika, Thakurmar Jhuli* and stories related to *Gopal Bhar*.

The musical tradition of Bangladesh is lyrics-based (*Baniprodhan*), with minimal instrumental accompaniment. The Baul tradition is a unique heritage of Bangla folk music, and there are numerous other musical traditions in Bangladesh, varying from one region to region. Gombhira, Bhatiali, Bhawaiya are a few of the better-known musical forms. Folk music of Bengal is often accompanied by the ektara, an instrument with only one string. Other instruments include the dotara, dhol, flute, and tabla. Bangladesh also has an active heritage in

North Indian classical music. Similarly, Bangladeshi dance forms draw from folk traditions, especially those of the tribal groups, as well as the broader Indian dance tradition.

Bangladesh produces about 80 films a year. Mainstream Hindi films are also quite popular. Around 200 daily newspapers are published in Bangladesh, along with more than 1800 periodicals. However, regular readership is low at just under 15% of the population. Bangladeshis listen to a variety of local and national radio programmes from Bangladesh Betar, as well as four Private FM radio channels (Radio Foorti, ABC Radio, Radio Today, Radio Amar) popularity to the younger generation is growing rapidly at the important cities. Also, there is Bangla services of Radio from the BBC and Voice of America. The dominant television channel is the state-controlled Bangladesh Television, but in the last few years, privately owned channels have developed considerably.

The culinary tradition of Bangladesh has close relations to Indian and Middle Eastern cuisine as well as having its own unique traits. Rice, and curry are traditional favourites. Bangladeshis make distinctive sweetmeats from milk products, some common ones being *Rôshogolla, chômchôm* and *kalojam*.

The sari *(shari)* is by far the most widely worn dress by Bangladeshi women. Dhaka in particular is renowned for producing saris from exquisite Jamdani muslin. The salwar kameez *(shaloar kamiz)* is also quite popular, and in urban areas some women wear Western attire. Among men, Western attire is more widely adopted. Men also wear the *kurta-paejama* combination, often on religious occasions, and the lungi, a kind of long skirt.

The two Eids, Eid ul-Fitr and Eid ul-Adha are the largest festivals in the Islamic calendar. The day before Eid ul-Fitr is called *Chãd Rat* (the night of the moon), often celebrated with firecrackers. Other Muslim holidays are also observed. Major Hindu festivals are Durga Puja, Kali puja and Saraswati Puja. Buddha Purnima, which marks the birth of Gautama Buddha, is one of the most important Buddhist festivals while Christmas, called *Bôrodin* (Great day) in Bangla is celebrated by the minority Christian population. The most important secular festival is Pohela Baishakh or Bengali New Year, the beginning of the Bengali calendar. Other festivities include Nobanno, *Poush parbon* (festival of Poush) and observance of national days like Shohid Dibosh.

Kabbadi is the national game of Bangladesh. Cricket and Football are more popular, with Cricket being the most popular sport in Bangladesh closely followed by Football. The Bangladesh national cricket team won the ICC Trophy in 1997 against Kenya which enabled them to participate in the 1999 Cricket World Cup. In their very first World Cup, Bangladesh beat The Pakistan and The Scotland in the first round. In 2000, the Bangladesh national cricket team was granted Test cricket status and became eligible to play other test playing nations.

At various times Bangladesh has beaten Australia, New Zealand, Sri Lanka, Pakistan, India, South Africa, Zimbabwe, and West Indies; more importantly Bangladesh beat The Indian national cricket team and The South African national cricket team in The 2007 Cricket World Cup. They have also beaten The West Indies in The 2007 ICC World Twenty20. In July 2009 The Bangladesh Cricket Team secured only its second Test Series win against The West Indies. The first one was against The Zimbabwean Cricket Team in the 2004–2005 season. In July 2010, Bangladesh enjoyed it's first ever win over England,in any form of the game,in a One Day International.

Other popular sports include field hockey, tennis, badminton, handball, volleyball, chess, shooting and carrom games. The Bangladesh Sports Control Board regulates twenty-nine different sporting federations. In 2011, Bangladesh is going to host the ICC Cricket World Cup jointly with India and Sri Lanka.

Bangladesh became one of the large nation states in 1971 when it seceded from Pakistan. Prior to the creation of Pakistan in 1947, modern-day Bangladesh was part of ancient, classical, medieval and colonial India. Since independence, the government has experienced periods of democratic and military rule. The founding leader of the country and its first president was Sheikh Mujibur Rahman. His daughter Sheikh Hasina Wazed is currently the prime minister, as leader of the Awami League. The opposition Bangladesh Nationalist Party is led by Begum Khaleda Zia, who is the widow of the revered freedom fighter and former president Ziaur Rahman.

The exact origin of the word *Bangla* or Bengal is unknown, though it is believed to be derived from the Dravidian-speaking tribe *Bang/Banga* that settled in the area around the year 1000 BCE. Other accounts speculate that the name is derived from *Vanga* (*Bôngo*), which came from the Austric word "Bonga" meaning the Sun-god. According to Mahabharata, Purana, Harivamsha Vanga was one of the adopted sons of king Vali who founded the Vanga kingdom. The Muslim Accounts refer that "Bong", a son of Hind (son of Ham who was a son of Prophet Noah/Nooh) colonized the area for the first time. The earliest reference to "Vangala" (*Bôngal*) has been traced in the Nesari plates (805 AD) of Rashtrakuta Govinda III which speak of Dharmapala as the king of Vangala. Shams-ud-din Ilyas Shah took the title "Shah-e-Bangalah" and united the whole region under one government for the first time. , Suhma Kingdom, and Vanga Kingdom

Pre-historic Bengal

Stone tools provide the earliest evidence of human settlements. Prehistoric stone implements have been discovered in various parts of West Bengal in the districts of Midnapur, Bankura and Burdwan. But it is difficult to determine, even approximately, the time when people using them first settled in Bengal. It might have taken place ten thousand years (or even more) ago. The original settlers spoke non-Aryan languages—they may have spoken Austric or Austro-Asiatic languages like the languages of the present-day Kola, Bhil, Santal, Shabara and Pulinda peoples. At a subsequent age, peoples speaking languages from two other language families—Dravidian and Tibeto-Burman—seem to have settled in Bengal. Archaeological discoveries during the 1960s furnished evidence of a degree of civilisation in certain parts of Bengal as far back as the beginning of the first millennium BC, perhaps even earlier. The discoveries at Pandu Rajar Dhibi in the valley of the Ajay River (near Bolpur) in Burdwan district and in several other sites on the Ajay, Kunar and Kopai Rivers have thrown fresh light on Bengal's prehistory. Pandu Rajar Dhibi represents the ruins of a trading township, which carried on trade not only with the interior regions of India, but also—possibly indirectly—with the countries of the Mediterranean.

Some deprecatory references indicate that the early people in Bengal were different in ethnicity and culture from the Vedic beyond the boundary of Aryandom and who were classed as 'Dasyus'. The Bhagavata Purana classes them as sinful people while Dharmasutra of Bodhayana prescribes expiatory rites after a journey among the Pundras and Vangas. Mahabharata speaks of Paundraka Vasudeva who was lord of the Pundrasand who allied himself with Jarasandha against Krishna. Mahabharata also speaks of Bengali kings called Chitrasena and Sanudrasena who were defeated by Bhima, Kalidas mentions Raghu defeated a coalition of Vanga kings who were defeated by Raghu and Raghu established a victory

Hindu scriptures such as the Mahabharata say that Bangladesh was divided among various tribes or kingdoms, including the Nishadas and kingdoms known as the Janapadas: Vanga (southern Bengal), Pundra (northern Bengal), and Suhma (western Bengal) according to their respective totems. These Hindu sources, written by Indo-Aryans in what is now Punjab and Uttar Pradesh, say that the peoples of Bangladesh were not Indo-Aryans. However, Jain scriptures identify Vanga and Anga in Bangladesh as Indo-Aryan. While western Bangladesh, as part of Magadha, became part of the Indo-Aryan civilization by the 7th century BCE, the Nanda Dynasty was the first historical state to unify all of Bangladesh under Indo-Aryan rule.

Overseas Colonization

The Vanga Kingdom was a powerful seafaring nation of Ancient India. They had overseas trade relations with Java,

Sumatra and Siam (modern day Thailand). According to Mahavamsa, the Vanga prince Vijaya Singha conquered Lanka (modern day Sri Lanka) in 544 BC and gave the name "Sinhala" to the country. Bengali people migrated to the Maritime South-east Asia and Siam (in modern Thailand), establishing their own colonies there.

Though north and west Bengal were part of the Magadhan empire southern Bengal thrived and became powerful with her overseas trades. In 326 BCE, with the invasion of Alexander the Great the region again came to prominence. The Greek and Latin historians suggested that Alexander the Great withdrew from India anticipating the valiant counter attack of the mighty Gangaridai empire that was located in the Bengal region. Alexander, after the meeting with his officer, Coenus, was convinced that it was better to return. Diodorus Siculus mentions Gangaridai to be the most powerful empire in India whose king possessed an army of 20,000 horses, 200,000 infantry, 2,000 chariots and 4,000 elephants trained and equipped for war. The allied forces of Gangaridai Empire and Nanda Empire (Prasii) were preparing a massive counter attack against the forces of Alexander on the banks of Ganges. Gangaridai according to the Greek accounts kept on flourishing at least up to the 1st century AD.

The pre-Gupta period of Bengal is shrouded with obscurity. Before the conquest of Samudragupta Bengal was divided into two kingdoms: Pushkarana and Samatata. Chandragupta II had defeated a confederacy of Vanga kings resulting in Bengal becoming part of the Gupta Empire.

Gauda Kingdom

By the sixth century, the Gupta Empire ruling over the northern Indian subcontinent was largely broken up. Eastern Bengal became the Vanga Kingdom while the Gauda kings rose in the west with their capital at Karnasuvarna (Murshidabad). Shashanka, a vassal of the last Gupta Empire became independent and unified the smaller principalities of Bengal (Gaur,

Vanga, Samatata) and vied for regional power with Harshavardhana in northern India. But this burst of Bengali power did not last beyond his death, as Bengal descended afterwards into a period marked by disunity and foreign invasion.

Pala dynasty were the first independent Buddhist dynasty of Bengal. The name *Pala* (Modern Bengali: ??? *pal*) means *protector* and was used as an ending to the names of all Pala monarchs. The Palas were followers of the Mahayana and Tantric schools of Buddhism. Gopala was the first ruler from the dynasty. He came to power in 750 in Gaur by a democratic election. This event is recognized as one of the first democratic elections in South Asia since the time of the Maha Janapadas. He reigned from 750-770 and consolidated his position by extending his control over all of Bengal. The Buddhist dynasty lasted for four centuries (750-1120 AD) and ushered in a period of stability and prosperity in Bengal. They created many temples and works of art as well as supported the Universities of Nalanda and Vikramashila. Somapura Mahavihara built by Dharmapala is the greatest Buddhist Vihara in the Indian Subcontinent.

The empire reached its peak under Dharmapala and Devapala. Dharmapala extended the empire into the northern parts of the Indian Subcontinent. This triggered once more for the control of the subcontinent. Devapala, successor of Dharmapala, expanded the empire to cover much of South Asia and beyond. His empire stretched from Assam and Utkala in the east, Kamboja (modern day Afghanistan) in the north-west and Deccan in the south. According to Pala copperplate inscription Devapala exterminated the Utkalas, conquered the Pragjyotisha (Assam), shattered the pride of the Huna, and humbled the lords of Gurjara, Pratiharas and the Dravidas.

The death of Devapala ended the period of ascendancy of the Pala Empire and several independent dynasties and kingdoms emerged during this time. However, Mahipala I rejuvenated the reign of the Palas. He recovered control over all of

Bengal and expanded the empire. He survived the invasions of Rajendra Chola and the Chalukyas. After Mahipala I the Pala dynasty again saw its decline until Ramapala, the last great ruler of the dynasty, managed to retrieve the position of the dynasty to some extent. He crushed the Varendra rebellion and extended his empire farther to Kamarupa, Orissa and Northern India.

The Pala Empire can be considered as the golden era of Bengal. Never had the Bengali people reached such height of power and glory to that extent. Palas were responsible for the introduction of Mahayana Buddhism in Tibet, Bhutan and Myanmar. The Pala had extensive trade as well as influence in south-east Asia. This can be seen in the sculptures and architectural style of the Sailendra Empire (present-day Malaya, Java, Sumatra).

The Palas were followed by the Sena dynasty who brought Bengal under one ruler during the twelfth century. Vijay Sen the second ruler of this dynasty defeated the last Pala emperor Madanapala and established his reign. Ballal Sena introduced caste system in Bengal and made Nabadwip the capital. The fourth king of this dynasty Lakshman Sen expanded the empire beyond Bengal to Bihar. Lakshman fled to eastern Bengal under the onslaught of the Muslims without facing them in battle. The Sena dynasty brought a brief period of revival of Hinduism in bengal. A popular myth comprehended by some Bengali authors about Jayadeva, the famous Sanskrit poet of Odisha(then known as the Kalingan Empire)and author of Gita Govinda, was one of the *Pancharatnas* (meaning 5 gems) in the court of Lakshman Sen.It remains a myth though as there remains no evidence to suggest so.

Late Middle Ages - arrival of Islam

Islam made its first appearance in Bengal during the twelfth century AD when Sufi missionaries arrived. Later occasional Muslim invaders reinforced the process of conversion by building mosques, madrassas and Sufi Khanqah. Beginning in 1202 a military commander from the Delhi Sultanate, Bakhtiar Khilji, overran Bihar and Bengal as far east as Rangpur, Bogra and the Brahmaputra River. The defeated Laksman Sen and his two sons moved to a place then called Vikramapur (present-day Munshiganj District), where their diminished dominion lasted until the late thirteenth century.Hindu bengali kingdoms continued to exist in the Southern nd the Eastern parts of Bengal till the 1450s.After the 1450s even they were overwhelmed by the Turkish attacks.Only Koch kingdom in the North could resist the Turks and later the Afghans,through the 1500s and the 1600s and weathered the Mughals also and survived till the advent of the British.Henceforth Hindu political power was thus limited to warlords and barons serving under Muslim kings,especially in the areas now in West Bengal and the western parts of Bangladesh.

The period after Bakhtiar Khilji's death in 1206 devolved into infighting among the Khiljis - representative of a pattern of succession struggles and intra-empire intrigues during later Turkic regimes. Ghiyasuddin Iwaz Khalji prevailed and extended the Sultan's domain south to Jessore and made the eastern Bang province a tributary. The capital was made at Lakhnauti on the Ganges near the older Bengal capital of Gaur. He managed to make Kamarupa and Trihut pay tribute to him. But he was later defeated by Shams-ud-Din Iltutmish.

Mameluk Rule

The weak successors of Iltutmish encouraged the local governors to declare independence. Bengal was sufficiently remote from Delhi that its governors would declare independence on occasion, styling themselves as Sultans of Bengal. It was during this time that Bengal earned the name "Bulgakpur" (land of the rebels). Tughral Togun Khan added Oudh and Bihar to Bengal. Mughisuddin Yuzbak also conquered Bihar and Oudh from Delhi but was killed during an unsuccessful expedition in Assam. Two Turkic attempts to push east of the broad Jamuna and Brahmaputra rivers were repulsed, but a third led by Mughisuddin Tughral conquered the Sonargaon area south of

Dhaka to Faridpur, bringing the Sen Kingdom officially to an end by 1277. Mughisuddin Tughral repulsed two massive attacks of the sultanate of Delhi before finally being defeated and killed by Ghiyas ud din Balban.

Mahmud Shahi Dynasty

Mahmud Shahi dynasty started when Nasiruddin Bughra Khan declared independence in Bengal. Thus Bengal regained her independence back. Nasiruddin Bughra Khan and his successors ruled Bengal for 23 years finally being incorporated into Delhi Sultanate by Ghyiasuddin Tughlaq .

Shamsuddin Iliyas Shah founded an independent dynasty that lasted from 1342-1487. The dynasty successfully repulsed attempts by Delhi to conquer them. They continued to reel in the territory of modern-day Bengal, reaching to Khulna in the south and Sylhet in the east. The sultans advanced civic institutions and became more responsive and "native" in their outlook and cut loose from Delhi. Considerable architectural projects were completed including the massive Adina Mosque and the Darasbari Mosque which still stands in Bangladesh near the border. The Sultans of Bengal were patrons of Bengali literature and began a process in which Bengali culture and identity would flourish. The Ilyas Shahi Dynasty was interrupted by an uprising by the Hindus under Raja Ganesha. However the Ilyas Shahi dynasty was restored by Nasiruddin Mahmud Shah. The dynasty was finally overthrown by the Habshi (Abyssinian) slaves of the sultanate.

Hussain Shahi Dynasty

The Habshi rule gave way to the Hussain Shahi dynasty that ruled from 1494-1538. Alauddin Hussain Shah, considered as the greatest of all the sultans of Bengal for bringing cultural renaissance during his reign. He extended the sultanate all the way to the port of Chittagong, which witnessed the arrival of the first Portuguese merchants. Nasiruddin Nasrat Shah gave refuge to the Afghan lords during the invasion of Babur though he remained neutral. However Nusrat Shah made a treaty with Babur and saved Bengal from a Mughal invasion. The last Sultan of the dynasty, who continued to rule from Gaur, had to contend with rising Afghan activity on his northwestern border. Eventually, the Afghans broke through and sacked the capital in 1538 where they remained for several decades until the arrival of the Mughals.

Sher Shah Suri established the Sur dynasty in Bengal. After the battle of Chausa he declared himself independent Sultan of Bengal and Bihar. Sher Shah was the only Muslim Sultan of Bengal to establish an empire in northern India. The Delhi Sultanate Islam Shah appointed Muhammad Khan Sur as the governor of Bengal. After the death of Islam Shah, Muhammad Khan Sur became independent. Muhammad Khan Sur was followed by Ghyiasuddin Bahadur Shah and Ghyiasuddin Jalal Shah. The Pashtun rule in Bengal remained for 44 years. Their most impressive achievement was Sher Shah's construction of the Grand Trunk Road connecting Sonargaon, Delhi and Peshawar.

Karrani Dynasty

The Sur dynasty was followed by the Karrani dynasty. Sulaiman Khan Karrani annexed Orissa to the Muslim sultanate permanently. Daoud Shah Karrani declared independence from Akbar which led to four years of bloody war between the Mughals and the Pashtuns. The Mughal onslaught against the Pashtun Sultan ended with the battle of Rajmahal in 1576, led by Khan Jahan. However, the Pashtun and the local landlords (Baro Bhuyans) led by Isa Khan resisted the Mughal invasion.

Bengal came once more under the control of Delhi as the Mughals conquered it in 1576. At that time Dhaka became a Mughal provincial capital. But it remained remote and thus a difficult to govern the region especially the section east of the Brahmaputra River remained outside the mainstream of Mughal politics. The Bengali ethnic and linguistic identity further crystallized during this period, since the whole of Bengal was united under an able and long-lasting administration. Furthermore its inhabitants were given sufficient autonomy to cultivate their own customs and literature.

In 1612, during Emperor Jahangir's reign, the defeat of Sylhet completed the Mughal conquest of Bengal with the exception of Chittagong. At this time Dhaka rose in prominence by becoming the provincial capital of Bengal. Chittagong was later annexed in order to stifle Arakanese raids from the east. A well-known Dhaka landmark, Lalbagh Fort, was built during Aurangzeb's sovereignty.

History repeated itself as the frontier Bengal province broke off from a Delhi-based empire around the time Aurangzeb's death in 1707. Murshid Quli Khan ended Dhaka's century of grandeur as he shifted the capital to Murshidabad ushering in a series of independent Bengal Nawabs. Nawab Alivardi Khan showed military skill during his wars with the Marathas. He completely routed the Marathas from Bengal. He crushed an uprising of the Afghans in Bihar and made the British pay 150,000 Tk for blocking Mughal and Armenian trade ships.

Portuguese traders and missionaries were the first Europeans to reach Bengal in the latter part of the fifteenth century. They were followed by representatives from the Netherlands, France, and the British East India Company. The Mughal Subahdar of Bengal Kasim Khan Mashadi completely destroyed the Portuguese forces in the Battle of Hoogly (1632). About 10,000 Portuguese men and women died in the battle and 4,400 were sent captive to Delhi.

During Aurangzeb's reign, the local Nawab sold three villages, including one then known as Calcutta, to the British. Calcutta was Britain's first foothold in Bengal and remained a focal point of their economic activity. The British gradually extended their commercial contacts and administrative control beyond Calcutta to the rest of Bengal. Job Charnock was one of the first dreamers of a British empire in Bengal. He waged war against the Mughal authority of Bengal which led to the Anglo-Mughal war for Bengal (1686–1690). Shaista Khan, the Nawab of Bengal, defeated the British in the battles of Hoogly as well as Baleshwar and expelled the British from Bengal. Captain William Heath with a naval fleet moved towards Chittagong but it was a failure and he had to retreat to Madras.

The British East India Company gained official control of Bengal following the Battle of Plassey in 1757. This was the first conquest, in a series of engagements that ultimately lead to the expulsion of other European competitors. The defeat of the Mughals and the consolidation of the subcontinent under the rule of a corporation was a unique event in imperialistic history. Kolkata (Anglicized as "Calcutta") on the Hooghly became a major trading port for bamboo, tea, sugar cane, spices, cotton, muslin and jute produced in Dhaka, Rajshahi, Khulna, and Kushtia.

Scandals and the bloody rebellion known as the Sepoy Mutiny prompted the British government to intervene in the affairs of the East India Company. In 1858, authority in India was transferred from the Company to the crown, and the rebellion was brutally suppressed. Rule of India was organized under a Viceroy and continued a pattern of economic exploitation. Famine racked the subcontinent many times, including at least two major famines in Bengal. The British Raj was politically organized into seventeen provinces of which Bengal was one of the most significant. For a brief period in the early twentieth century, an abortive attempt was made to divide Bengal into two zones, West Bengal and East Bengal & Assam.

As the independence movement throughout British-controlled India began in the late nineteenth century gained momentum during the twentieth century, Bengali politicians played an active role in Mohandas Gandhi's Congress Party and Mohammad Ali Jinnah's Muslim League, exposing the opposing forces of ethnic and religious nationalism. By exploiting the latter, the British probably intended to distract the independence movement, for example by partitioning Bengal in 1905 along religious lines. The split only lasted for seven years.

At first the Muslim League sought only to ensure minority rights in the future nation. In 1940 the Muslim League passed the Lahore Resolution which envisaged one or more Muslim majority states in South Asia. Non-negotiable was the inclusion of the Muslim parts of Punjab and Bengal in these proposed states. The stakes grew as a new Viceroy Lord Mountbatten of Burma was appointed expressly for the purpose of effecting a graceful British exit. Communal violence in Noakhali and Calcutta sparked a surge in support for the Muslim League, which won a majority of Bengal's Muslim seats in the 1946 election. Accusations have been made that Hindu and Muslim nationalist instigators were involved in the latter incident. At the last moment Huseyn Shaheed Suhrawardy and Sarat Chandra Bose came up with the idea of an independent and unified Bengal state, which was endorsed by Jinnah. This idea was vetoed by the Indian National Congress.

British India was partitioned and the independent states of India and Pakistan were created in 1947; the region of Bengal was divided along religious lines. The predominantly Muslim eastern half of Bengal became the East Bengal (later renamed East Pakistan) state of Pakistan and the predominantly Hindu western part became the Indian state of West Bengal.

Pakistan's history from 1947 to 1971 was marked by political instability and economic difficulties. In 1956 a constitution was at last adopted, making the country an "Islamic republic within the Commonwealth". The nascent democratic institutions foundered in the face of military intervention in 1958, and the government imposed martial law between 1958 and 1962, and again between 1969 and 1971.

Almost from the advent of independent Pakistan in 1947, frictions developed between East and West Pakistan, which were separated by more than 1,000 miles of Indian territory. East Pakistanis felt exploited by the West Pakistan-dominated central government. Linguistic, cultural, and ethnic differences also contributed to the estrangement of East from West Pakistan.

When Mohammad Ali Jinnah died in September 1948, Khwaja Nazimuddin became the Governor General of Pakistan while Nurul Amin was appointed the Chief Minister of East Bengal. Nurul Amin continued as the Chief Minister of East Bengal until 2 April 1954. The abolition of the Zamindari system in East Bengal (1950) and the Language Movement were two most important events during his tenure.

The question as to what would be the state language of Pakistan was raised immediately after its creation. The central leaders and the Urdu-speaking intellectuals of Pakistan declared that Urdu would be the state language of Pakistan, just as Hindi was the state language of India. However, Bengalis strongly resisted attempts to impose Urdu as the sole official language of Pakistan, and the students and intellectuals of East Pakistan, demanded that Bengali (Bangla) be made one of the state languages, arguing that it was in any case the native language of the majority (54% native speakers as opposed to 7% native Urdu speakers) in the whole of Pakistan.

The Bengali Language Movement began in 1948 and reached its climax in a demonstration on 21 February 1952 at which several demonstrators were killed by police. After a lot of controversy over the language issue, the final demand from East Pakistan was that Bangla must be the official language and the medium of instruction in East Pakistan, and that for the central government it would be one of the state languages along with Urdu. The first movement on this issue was mobilised by Tamaddun Majlish headed by Professor Abul Kashem. Gradually many other non-communal and progressive organisations joined the movement, which finally turned into a mass movement, and ended in the adoption of Bengali as one of the state languages of Pakistan.

The first election for East Bengal Provincial Assembly was held between 8 March and 12 March 1954. The Awami Muslim League, Krishak-Sramik Party and Nezam-e-Islam formed the United Front, on the basis of 21-points agenda.

Notable pledges contained in the 21-points were:

making Bengali one of the main state languages
autonomy for the province
reforms in education
independence of the judiciary
making the legislative assembly effective

The United Front won 215 out of 237 Muslim seats in the election. The ruling Muslim League got only nine seats. Khilafat-E-Rabbani Party got one, while the independents got twelve seats. Later, seven independent members joined the United Front while one joined the Muslim League.

There were numerous reasons for the debacle of the Muslim League. Above all, the Muslim League regime angered all sections of the people of Bengal by opposing the demand for recognition of Bangla as one of the state languages and by ordering the massacre of 1952.

The United Front got the opportunity to form the provincial government after winning absolute majority in the 1954 election. Of the 222 United Front seats, the Awami Muslim League had won 142, Krishak-Sramik Party 48, Nezam-i-Islam 19, and Ganatantri Dal 13.

The major leaders of the United Front were Huseyn Shaheed Suhrawardy and Maulana Abdul Hamid Khan Bhasani of Awami Muslim League and A. K. Fazlul Huq of Krishak-Sramik Party. Suhrawardy and Bhasani did not take part in the election and Fazlul Huq was invited to form the government. But a rift surfaced at the very outset on the question of formation of the cabinet. The unity and solidarity among the component parties of the United Front soon evaporated. Finally, on 15 May, Fazlul Huq arrived at an understanding with the Awami Muslim League and formed a 14-member cabinet with five members from that party.

But this cabinet lasted for only fourteen days. The Muslim League could not concede defeat in the elections in good grace. So, they resorted to conspiracies to dismiss the United Front government. In the third week of May, there were bloody riots between Bengali and non-Bengali workers in different mills and factories of East Bengal. The United Front government was blamed for failing to control the law and order situation in the province.

Fazlul Huq was then quoted in an interview taken by *The New York Times* correspondent John P Callaghan and published in a distorted form that he wanted the independence of East Bengal. Finally, on 29 May 1954, the United Front government was dismissed by the central government and Governor's rule was imposed in the province, which lasted till 2 June 1955.

Curiously enough within two months of his sacking, Fazlul Huq was appointed the central Home Minister. As Home Minister, Fazlul Huq utilised his influence to bring his party to power in East Bengal. Naturally, the United Front broke up. The Muslim members of the United Front split into two groups. In 1955 the Awami Muslim League adopted the path of secularism and non-communalism, erased the word 'Muslim' from its nomenclature and adopted the name "Awami League".

Great differences began developing between the two wings of Pakistan. While the west had a minority share of Pakistan's total population, it had the largest share of revenue allocation, industrial development, agricultural reforms and civil development projects. Pakistan's military and civil services were dominated by the fair-skinned, Persian-cultured Punjabis and Afghans. Only one regiment in the Pakistani Army was Bengali. And many Bengali Pakistanis could not share the natural enthusiasm for the Kashmir issue, which they felt was leaving East Pakistan more vulnerable and threatened as a result.

After the Awami League won all the East Pakistan seats of the Pakistan's National Assembly in the 1970-71 elections, West Pakistan opened talks with the East on constitutional questions about the division of power between the central government and the provinces, as well as the formation of a national government headed by the Awami League.

The talks proved unsuccessful, however, and on March 1, 1971, Pakistani President Yahya Khan indefinitely postponed the pending National Assembly session, precipitating massive civil disobedience in East Pakistan.

On March 2, 1971, a group of students, led by A S M Abdur Rob, student leader & VP of DUCSU (Dhaka University Central Students Union) raised the new (proposed) flag of Bangla under the direction of Swadhin Bangla.

On March 3, 1971, student leader Sahjahan Siraj read the Sadhinotar Ishtehar (Declaration of independence) at Paltan Maidan in front of Bangabandhu Shaikh Mujib along with student and public gathering.

On March 7, there was a historical public gathering in Paltan Maidan to hear the guideline for the revolution and independence from Shaikh Mujib, the frontier leader of movement that time. Although he avoided the direct speech of independence as the talks were still underway, he influenced the mob to prepare for the separation war. The speech is still considered a key moment in the war of liberation, and is remembered for the phrase, "Ebarer Shongram Muktir Shongram, Ebarer Shongram Shadhinotar Shongram...." ("This time, the revolution is for freedom; this time, the revolution is for liberation....")

After the military crackdown by the Pakistan army began on the night of March 25, 1971 Bangabandhu Sheikh Mujibur Rahman was arrested and the political leaders dispersed, mostly fleeing to neighbouring India where they organized a provisional government afterwards. Before being held up by the Pakistani Army Sheikh Mujibur Rahman gave a hand note of the declaration of the independence of Bangladesh and it was circulated amongst people and transmitted by the then East Pakistan Rifles' wireless transmitter. Bengali Army Major Zia-Ur-Rahman captured Kalurghat Radio Station in Chittagong and read the declaration of independence of Bangladesh. On 27th march Major Zia read the declaration of independence on behalf of Sheikh Mujibur Rahman, "I, Major Zia-ur-Rahman, who hereby declare the independence of Bangladesh, on behalf of our great national leader Bangabandhu Sheikh Mujibur Rahman".

The Provisional Government of the People's Republic of Bangladesh was formed in Meherpur, (later renamed as Mujibnagar a place adjacent to the Indian Border). Sheikh Mujibur Rahman was announced to be the head of the state. Tajuddin Ahmed became the prime minister of the government. There the war plan was sketched. A war force was established named "Muktibahini". M. A. G. Osmani was assigned as the Chief of the force. The land sketched into 11 sectors under 11 sector commanders. Along with this sectors on the later part of the war Three special forces were formed namely Z Force, S Force and K Force. These three forces name were derived from the initial letter of the commandar's name. The training and most of the arms-ammunitions were arranged by the Meherpur government which were supported by India. As fighting grew between the Pakistan Army and the Bengali Mukti Bahini ("freedom fighters"), an estimated ten million Bengalis, mainly Hindus, sought refuge in the Indian states of Assam, Tripura and West Bengal.

The crisis in East Pakistan produced new strains in Pakistan's troubled relations with India. The two nations had fought a war in 1965, mainly in the west, but the refugee pressure in India in the fall of 1971 produced new tensions in the east. Indian sympathies lay with East Pakistan, and on December 3, 1971, India intervened on the side of the Bangladeshis. On December 16, 1971, Pakistani forces surrendered, and Bangla Desh ("Country of Bangla") was finally established the following day. The new country changed its name to Bangladesh on January 11, 1972 and became a parliamentary democracy under a constitution. Shortly thereafter on March 19 Bangladesh signed a friendship treaty with India.

Sheikh Mujibur Rahman came to office with immense personal popularity but had difficulty transforming this popular support into the political strength needed to function as head of government. The 1972 constitution adopted as state policy the Awami League (AL) four basic principles of nationalism, secularism, socialism, and democracy.

The first parliamentary elections were held in March 1973, with the Awami League winning a massive majority. The new Bangladesh government focused on relief, rehabilitation, and reconstruction of the economy and society. In December 1974, in the face of continuing economic deterioration and mounting civil disorder, Mujib proclaimed a state of emergency, limited the powers of the legislative and judicial branches, banned all the newspaper except four government supported papers, and introduced one-party system baning all the other parties.

Despite some improvement in the economic situation during the first half of 1975, criticism of Mujib grew. In August 1975, Mujib, and most of his family, were assassinated by mid-level army officers. A new government, headed by former Mujib associate Khandakar Moshtaque Ahmed, was formed

Successive military coups resulted in the emergence of Army Chief of Staff Gen. Ziaur Rahman ("Zia") as strongman. In the historic 7 November 1975, "Jatiyo Biplob O Shanghoti Dibosh" the army captured the power freed Major Zia. He pledged the army's support to the civilian government headed by President Chief Justice Sayem. Acting at Zia's behest, Sayem dissolved Parliament, and instituted the Martial Law Administration (MLA).

In November 1976, Zia became Chief Martial Law Administrator (CMLA) and assumed the presidency upon Sayem's forced retirement five months later, promising national elections in 1978.

As President, Zia announced a 19-point program of economic reform and began dismantling the MLA. Zia won a five-year term in June 1978 elections, with 76% of the vote. Democracy and constitutional order were fully restored when the ban on political parties was lifted, new parliamentary elections were held in February 1979. The AL and the Bangladesh Nationalist Party (BNP), founded by Zia, emerged as the two major parties.

In May 1981, Zia was assassinated in Chittagong by dissident elements of the military. The conspirators were either taken into custody or killed. Vice-President Justice Abdus Sattar was sworn in as acting president, and elected president as the BNP's candidate six months later. Sattar followed the policies of his predecessor and retained essentially the same cabinet.

In March 1982 Army Chief of Staff Lt. Gen. H.M. Ershad suspended the constitution and declared martial law citing pervasive corruption, ineffectual government, and economic mismanagement. The following year, Ershad assumed the presidency, and won overwhelming public support for his regime in a national referendum in March 1985, although turnout was small. Political life was liberalized through 1985 and 1986, and the Jatiya (National) Party was established as Ershad's vehicle for the transition back to democracy.

Parliamentary elections were held in May 1986, but were boycotted by the BNP, now led by President Zia's widow, Begum Khaleda Zia. The Jatiya Party won a modest majority of the 300 elected seats in the National Assembly. The participation of the Awami League—led by the late President Mujib's daughter, Sheikh Hasina Wajed—lent the elections some credibility, despite widespread charges of voting irregularities.

Ershad retired from military service in preparation for the presidential elections in October 1986, and won 84% of the vote. Protesting that martial law was still in effect, both the BNP and the AL refused to put up opposing candidates. In November 1986, martial law was lifted, and the opposition parties took their elected seats in the National Assembly.

In July 1987, after the government hastily pushed through a bill to include military representation on local administrative councils, the opposition walked out of Parliament. As the opposition organized protest marches and nationwide strikes, the government arrested scores of opposition activists. After declaring a state of emergency, Ershad dissolved Parliament and scheduled fresh elections for March 1988.

The elections were held despite an opposition boycott, and the ruling Jatiya Party won 251 of the 300 seats. The Parliament passed a large number of bills, including in June 1988 a controversial constitutional amendment making Islam Bangladesh's state religion.

On December 6, 1990, following general strikes, increased campus protests, public rallies, and a general disintegration of law and order, Ershad resigned. On February 27, 1991, an interim government headed by Acting President Chief Justice Shahabuddin Ahmed oversaw what most observers believed to be the nation's most free and fair elections to that date.

BNP won a plurality of seats and formed a government with Khaleda Zia, widow of Ziaur Rahman, becoming prime minister. The electorate approved changes to the constitution, formally re-creating a In March 1994, controversy over a parliamentary by-election, which the opposition claimed the government had rigged, led to general strikes and an indefinite boycott of Parliament by the opposition. In late December 1994, the opposition resigned en masse from Parliament, and pledged to boycott national elections scheduled for February 15, 1996.

In February, Khaleda Zia was re-elected by a landslide in voting boycotted by the three main opposition parties. In March 1996, following escalating political turmoil, the Parliament amended the constitution to allow a neutral caretaker government to assume power and conduct new parliamentary elections.

Sheikh Hasina, 1996-2001

Elections were held in June 1996 which were found by international and domestic election observers to be free and fair. The Awami League won a plurality of the seats, and formed the government with support from the Jatiya Party of deposed president Ershad. AL leader Sheikh Hasina became Prime Minister.

In June 1999, the BNP and other opposition parties again began to boycott Parliament, and stage nationwide general strikes. A four-party opposition alliance formed at the beginning of 1999 announced that it would boycott parliamentary by-elections and local government.

Four Party Aliiance led by BNP, 2001-2006

The four-party alliance led by the Bangladesh Nationalist Party (BNP) won over a two-thirds majority in Parliament. Begum Khaleda Zia was sworn in on October 10, 2001, as Prime Minister for the third time.

An grenade attack on a rally of Sheikh Hasina killed 23 people on August 21, 2004. On August 17, 2005, near-synchronized blasts of improvised explosive devices in 63 out of 64 administrative districts targeted mainly government buildings and killed two persons. An extremist Islamist group named Jama'atul Mujahideen, Bangladesh (JMB) claimed responsibility for the blasts, which aimed to press home JMB's demand for a replacement of the secular legal system with Islamic sharia courts. Hundreds of senior and mid-level JMB leaders were arrested.

In February 2006, after sporadic boycotts, the AL returned to Parliament, demanded early elections and requested significant changes in the electoral and caretaker government systems to stop alleged moves by the ruling coalition to rig the next election. Dialogue between the Secretaries General of the main ruling and opposition parties failed to sort out the electoral reform issues.

In July 2001, the Awami League government stepped down to allow a caretaker government to preside over parliamentary elections. In August, Khaleda Zia and Sheikh Hasina agreed to respect the results of the election, join Parliament win or lose, foreswear the use of hartals (violently enforced strikes) as political tools, and if successful in forming a government allow for a more meaningful role for the opposition in Parliament. The caretaker government was successful in containing the violence, which allowed a parliamentary end.

Caretaker Government, Oct 2006-Jan 2009

On January 3, 2007, the Awami League announced it would boycott the January 22 parliamentary elections. The AL planned a series of country-wide general strikes and transportation blockades.

On January 11, 2007, President Iajuddin Ahmed declared a state of emergency, resigned as Chief Adviser, and indefinitely postponed parliamentary elections. On January 12, 2007, former Bangladesh Bank governor Fakhruddin Ahmed was sworn in as the new Chief Adviser, and ten new advisers (ministers) were appointed. Under emergency provisions, the government suspended certain fundamental rights guaranteed by the constitution and detained a large number of politicians and others on suspicion of involvement in corruption and other crimes. The government announced elections would occur in late 2008. As of November 19, 2008, elections were scheduled for December 8, 2008.

In the summer of 2007 the government arrested Sheikh Hasina and Khaleda Zia, Bangladesh's two most influential political leaders, on charges of corruption. Hasina and Zia have challenged the cases filed against them under the Emergency Power Rules, which deny the accused the right to bail. While the cases are under judicial review, the two leaders continue to be imprisoned as of March 2008.

Grand Alliance January 2009-present

On 19 November 2008 Awami League & Jatiya Party agreed to contest the elections jointly under the Caretaker Government to be held on 29 December 2008. Out of the 300 Constituencies in the Parliament, Ershad's Jatiya Party will contest from 49 seats and Awami League and members of a *leftist wing* Fourteen Party Coalition from the rest 250 seats. Thus the Grand Alliance emerged in Bangladesh; known as *Mohajote* in Bangla

On December 29, 2008 Bangladesh went to the polls and the nation elected the Grand Alliance which was led by Sheikh

Hasina's Awami League and backed by Hussain Mohammed Ershad's Jatiya Party. On the other hand Khaleda Zia's BNP-led Four Party Alliance plagued by allegations of Khaleda Zia's and her infamous son Tareq Rahman's corruption allegations , suffered the most embarrassing defeat ever in Bangladesh's history.

Sheikh Hasina became Prime Minister and formed the government and a cabinet which included ministers from Jatiya Party although any post for Hussain Mohammed Ershad, is yet to be decided as the earlier agreed Presidency seems elusive.

The mutiny of borderguards (BDR) took place from 25 to 27 February 2009. More than a thousand BDR soldiers took over the BDR headquarters, and held many of their officers hostage. By the second day fighting spread to 12 other towns and cities. The mutiny ended as the mutineers surrendered their arms and released the hostages after a series of discussions and negotiations with the government. 52 army died in the incident.

10

BENGAL PRESIDENCY

The Bengal Presidency originally comprising east and west Bengal, was a colonial region of British India, which comprised undivided Bengal, which is present day Bangladesh and West Bengal, as well as the states Assam, Bihar, Meghalaya, Orissa and Tripura. Later at its height, gradually added, were the annexed princely states of Uttar Pradesh, Uttarakhand, Punjab in India, Haryana, and Himachal Pradesh and portions of Chhatisgarh, Madhya Pradesh, and Maharashtra in present day India, including the provinces of North West Frontier and Punjab in Pakistan, and Burma (present day Myanmar). Penang and Singapore were also considered to be administratively a part of the Presidency until they were incorporated into the Crown Colony of the Straits Settlements in 1867. Calcutta was declared a Presidency Town of the East India Company in 1699, but the beginnings of the Bengal Presidency proper can be dated from the treaties of 1765 between the East India Company and the Mughal Emperor and Nawab of Oudh which placed Bengal, Meghalaya, Bihar and Orissa under the administration of the Company. The Presidency of Bengal, in contradistinction to those of Madras and Bombay, eventually included all the British territories North of the Central Provinces (Madhya Pradesh), from the mouths of the Ganges and Brahmaputra to the Himalayas and the Punjab. In 1831 the North-Western Provinces were created, which were subsequently included with Oudh in the United Provinces (Uttar Pradesh); Just before the

First World War the whole of Northern India was divided into the four lieutenant-governorships of the Punjab, the United Provinces, Bengal, and Eastern Bengal and Assam, and the North-West Frontier Province under a Commissioner.

The name "Bengal" is derived from Sanskrit "Vanga", and, strictly speaking, applies to the country stretching southwards from Bhagalpur to the sea. The ancient Bangla formed one of the five outlying kingdoms of Aryan India, and was practically coterminous with the delta of Bengal. It derived its name, according to the etymology of the Pundits, from a prince of the Mahabharata, to whose portion it fell on the partition of the country among the Lunar race of Delhi. But a city called Bangala, near Chittagong, which, although now washed away, is supposed to have existed in the Muslim period, appears to have given the name to the European world. The word *Bangala* was first used by the Muslim rulers; and under their rule, like the Bangla pre-Muslim times, it applied specifically to the Gangetic delta, although the later conquests to the east of the Brahmaputra were eventually included within it. In their distribution of the country for fiscal purposes, it formed the central province of a governorship, with Bihar on the north-west, and Orissa on the south-west, jointly ruled by one deputy of the Delhi emperor. Under the English the name has at different periods borne very different significations. Francis Fernandez applies it to the country from the extreme east of Chittagong to Point Palmyras in Orissa, with a coast line which Purchas estimates at 600 m., running inland for the same distance and watered by the Ganges. This territory would include the Muslim province of Bengal, with parts of Bihar and Orissa. The loose idea thus derived from old voyagers became stereotyped in the archives of the East India Company. All its north-eastern factories, from Balasore, on the Orissa coast, to Patna, in the heart of Bihar, belonged to the Bengal Establishment, and as British conquests crept higher up the rivers, the term came to be applied to the whole of Northern India.

The East India Company formed its earliest settlements in Bengal in the first half of the 17th century. These settlements were of a purely commercial character. In 1620 one of the Company's factors was based in Patna; in 1624–1636 the Company established itself, by the favour of the emperor, on the ruins of the ancient Portuguese settlement of Pippli, in the north of Orissa; in 1640–1642 an English surgeon, Gabriel Boughton, obtained establishments at Balasore, also in Orissa, and at Hughli, some miles above Calcutta, where the Portuguese already had a settlement. The difficulties which the Company's early agents encountered more than once almost induced them to abandon the trade, and in 1677–1678 they threatened to withdraw from Bengal altogether. In 1685, the Bengal factors, seeking greater security for their trade purchased from the grandson of Aurangzeb, in 1696, the villages which have since grown up into Calcutta, the metropolis of India, namely Kalikata, Sutanuti and Govindpur. They were given exemption from trade duties and exactions in part of Bengal in 1717 by the Emperor Farrukhsiyar. During the next forty years the British had a long and hazardous struggle alike with the Mughal governors of the province and the Maratha armies which invaded it. In 1756 this struggle culminated in the fall of Calcutta to Nawab Siraj Ud Daulah followed by Clive's battle of Plassey and recapture of the city. The Battle of Buxar established British military supremacy in Bengal, and procured the treaties of 1765, by which the provinces of Bengal, Bihar and Orissa passed under British administration. The other important institution which emerged in this period was the Bengal Army.

Under Warren Hastings (British Governorships 1772-1785) the consolidation of British imperial rule over Bengal, and the conversion of mere trade into an entire military occupied territory under a military backed civil government got solidified. To another member of the civil service, John Shore, afterwards Lord Teignmouth, was due the formation of a regular system of legislation. Acting through Lord Cornwallis, then Governor-General, he ascertained and defined the rights of the landholders in the soil. These landholders under the previous system had started, for the most part, as collectors of the revenues, and gradually acquired certain prescriptive rights as quasi-proprietors of the estates entrusted to them by the government. In 1793 Lord Cornwallis declared their rights perpetual, and made over the land of Bengal to the previous quasi-proprietors or *zamindars*, on condition of the payment of a fixed land tax. This piece of legislation is known as the Permanent Settlement of the Land Revenue. It was designed to "introduce" ideas of property rights to India, and stimulate a market in land. The former aim misunderstood the nature of landholding in India, and the latter was an abject failure. The Cornwallis code, while defining the rights of the proprietors, failed to give adequate recognition to the rights of the under-tenants and the cultivators. This remained a serious problem for the duration of British Rule, as throughout the Bengal Presidency *ryots* (peasants) found themselves oppressed by rack-renting landlords, who knew that every rupee they could squeeze from their tenants over and above the fixed revenue demand from the Government represented pure profit. Furthermore the Permanent Settlement took no account of inflation, meaning that the value of the revenue to Government declined year by year, whilst the heavy burden on the peasantry grew no less. This was compounded in the early 19th century by compulsory schemes for the cultivation of Opium and Indigo, the former by the state, and the latter by British planters (most especially in the district of Tirhut in Bihar). Peasants were forced to grow a certain area of these crops, which were then purchased at below market rates for export. This added greatly to rural poverty.

So unsuccessful was the Permanent Settlement that it was not introduced in the North-Western Provinces (taken from the Marathas during the campaigns of Lord Lake and Arthur Wellesley) after 1831, in Punjab after its conquegal. The province of West Bengal then consisted of the thirty-three districts of Burdwan, Birbhum, Bankura, Midnapur, Hughli, Howrah, Twenty-four Parganas, Calcutta, Nadia, Murshidabad, Jessore,

Khulna, Patna, Gaya, Shahabad, Saran, Champaran, Muzaffarpur, Darbhanga, Monghyr, Bhagalpur, Purnea, Santhal Parganas, Cuttack, Balasore, Angul and Khondmals, Pun, Hazaribagh, Ranchi, Palamau, Manbhum, Singhbum and Sambalpur, and the princely states of Sikkim and the tributary states of Orissa and Chota Nagpur.

This decision proved highly controversial, as it resulted in a largely Hindu West Bengal and a largely Muslim East. Serious popular agitation followed this step, partly on the grounds that this was part of a cynical policy of divide and rule, and partly that the Bengali populat Malda District and the States of Hill Tripura, Sylhet and Comilla were transferred from Bengal to a new province, Eastern Bengal and Assam; the five Hindi-speaking states of Chota Nagpur, namely Chang Bhakar, Korea, Sirguja, Udaipur and Jashpur, were transferred from Bengal to the Central Provinces; and Sambalpur and the five Oriya states of Bamra, Rairakhol, Sonepur, Patna and Kalahandi were transferred from the Central Provinces to Bengal. The province of West Bengal then consisted of the thirty-three districts of Burdwan, Birbhum, Bankura, Midnapur, Hughli, Howrah, Twenty-four Parganas, Calcutta, Nadia, Murshidabad, Jessore, Khulna, Patna, Gaya, Shahabad, Saran, Champaran, Muzaffarpur, Darbhanga, Monghyr, Bhagalpur, Purnea, Santhal Parganas, Cuttack, Balasore, Angul and Khondmals, Pun, Hazaribagh, Ranchi, Palamau, Manbhum, Singhbum and Sambalpur, and the princely states of Sikkim and the tributary states of Orissa and Chota Nagpur.

This decision proved highly controversial, as it resulted in a largely Hindu West Bengal and a largely Muslim East. Serious popular agitation followed this step, partly on the grounds that this was part of a cynical policy of divide and rule, and partly that the Bengali population, the centre of whose interests and prosperity was Calcutta, would now be divided under two governments, instead of being concentrated and numerically dominant under the one, while the bulk would be in the new division. In 1906–1909 the unrest developed to a considerable extent, requiring special attention from the Indian and Home governments, and this led to the decision being reversed in 1912. The same year saw the separation from Bengal of Bihar and Orissa, later itself subdivided into the Province of Bihar and the Province of Orissa, the former with its capital at Patna, the latter administered from Cuttack. This change proved a popular and lasting one.

With this final partition, the Bengal Presidency ceased to exist in all but name, and even this disappeared after the Montagu-Chelmsford reforms of 1919 reconstituted Indian Provincial Government.